P9-DXK-439

3 9350 007336716

DATE DUE

JUN 1 5 2001
JUN 3 0 2001
JUL 0 6 2001

JAN 3 0 2002
FEB 1 3 2002
FEB 2 7 2002
APR 0 1 2002
APR 1 7 2002
MAY 1 6 2002

MAY 1 6 2001

Palos Verdes Library Distric

Switzerland

Switzerland

BY LURA ROGERS

Enchantment of the World
Second Series

Children's Press®

A Division of Scholastic Inc.

NEW YORK TORONTO LONDON AUCKLAND SYDNEY
MEXICO CITY NEW DELHI HONG KONG
DANBURY, CONNECTICUT·

Frontispiece: Decorative cowbells

Consultant: Thomas Ertman, Ph.D., Associate Professor of Sociology at New York University and an Affiliate of the Center for European Studies at Harvard University

Please note: *All statistics are as up-to-date as possible at the time of publication.*

Visit Children's Press on the Internet: http://publishing.grolier.com

Book Production by Herman Adler Design

Library of Congress Cataloging-in-Publication Data

Rogers, Lura
    Switzerland / by Lura Rogers.
      p. cm. — (Enchantment of the world. Second series)
    Includes bibliographical references and index.
    Summary: Describes the history, geography, plants and animals, economy, language, people, and culture of Switzerland.
    ISBN 0-516-21080-7
    1. Switzerland—Juvenile literature. [1. Switzerland.] I. Title. II. Series.
DQ17.R57 2001
949.4—dc21   99-056158

© 2001 by Children's Press®, a Division of Scholastic Inc.
All rights reserved. Published simultaneously in Canada.
Printed in the United States of America.

GROLIER PUBLISHING

1 2 3 4 5 6 7 8 9 10 R 10 09 08 07 06 05 04 03 02 01

Acknowledgments

The author would like to thank the reference staffs of the Saratoga Springs (New York) Public Library and the Keene (New Hampshire) Public Library, especially B. J. Nielsen, for their help with research. She is also grateful for the help of her editor, Halley Gatenby.

Contents

Cover photo:
Lake Geneva

Alphorns are a Swiss musical tradition.

The city of Bern

Triumph over Diversity

SWITZERLAND ROSE FROM A BEAUTIFUL BUT INHOSPITABLE landscape. By hard work, compromise, and a strong will to succeed, this small country has grown from a group of widely scattered settlements to one of the world's most prosperous nations. Along the way, the Swiss learned to be tolerant of the differences among their people.

Opposite: **The clock tower in Zürich, Switzerland's largest city**

Railways carry passengers up Switzerland's steep mountain slopes.

In spite of the fact that they are located between nations that were frequently at war, Switzerland has stayed out of most of Europe's wars by using their skills in diplomacy to keep them neutral. Switzerland's mountainous terrain has been a natural barrier in times of conflict.

Although they could never tame their mountains, the Swiss tunneled through them for transportation. They made a land with no mineral resources or seaport into a great industrial and trading nation. The Swiss imported raw materials from other countries and used them to create high-quality products. Their skill in business made Switzerland the banking capital of Europe.

SWITZERLAND

- ● Cities of over 100,000 people
- ◉ Cities of over 30,000 people
- ○ Smaller cities and towns

0   100 miles

0   150 kilometers

GERMANY

FRANCE

Schaffhausen

L. Constance

Rhine

Thur

Augst

AARGAU

St. Gallen

Basel

Baden

Limmat

ZÜRICH

THURGAU

Liestal

Sissach

Windisch

ST. GALLEN

Rhine

BASEL

Zürich

LIECHTENSTEIN

AUSTRIA

Aare

Reuss

JURA

ZUG

Einsiedeln

La Chaux-de-Fonds

BERN

Bolligen

LUCERNE

Lucerne

Vitznau

SCHWYZ

Braunwald

Neuchâtel

Köniz

Bern

L. Lucerne

Treib

GLARUS

NEUCHÂTEL

Fribourg

Thun

L. Sarnen

Altdorf

Burglen

Vorderrhein

Chur

Avenches

Riggisberg

Sachsein

Disentis-Müster

Orbe

FRIBOURG

Simme

Interlaken

GRAUBÜNDEN

Hinterrhein

Inn

Orbe

L. Thun

Lötschberg Tunnel

VAUD

Lausanne

Ticino

SWISS NATIONAL PARK

L. Geneva

Vevey-Montreux

Chillon

Rhone

Simplon Tunnel

GENEVA

Sion

VALAIS

Locarno

Geneva

St. Maurice

Zermatt

L. Maggiore

L. Como

ITALY

SWITZERLAND

N

W   E

S

Geopolitical map of
Switzerland

Switzerland is known for its art, architecture, music, and strong folk traditions. Each region has its own colorful, lively culture, celebrated in local festivals.

The Swiss made the snow-covered mountainsides a winter playground, connecting them with cable cars and special railways. Then they built beautiful hotels and resorts and invited the world to join the fun and enjoy their beautiful scenery.

Switzerland accomplished all this despite having four national languages and three major ethnic groups, in a country small enough to be contained in a circle with a radius of less than 71 miles (114.3 kilometers). Divided into 26 cantons, Switzerland's triumph over diversity is the key to its success, and to its leadership in the drive for worldwide peace and cooperation.

Girls in traditional costumes at a summer festival

What Is a Canton?

A canton is a state of the Swiss Confederation, and represents a political division.

Young skiers in a friendly competition

Perilous Peaks and Welcome Waters

SWITZERLAND IS SNUGLY NESTLED BETWEEN GERMANY, Austria, Italy, France, and Liechtenstein, with a border of 1,151 miles (1,852 km). The total area of the country is 15,942 square miles (41,284 square kilometer), which is about the size of New Jersey and Massachusetts combined. East to west, the maximum distance across Switzerland is 213 miles (343 km), and north to south it stretches only 138 miles (222 km). Its dominant mountain chains and its position in central Europe make Switzerland an important part of Europe.

Think of Switzerland and you think of mountains. The Alps and the Jura Mountains cover 70 percent of the country. The remaining 30 percent of land area is called the Mittelland, or the Swiss Plateau. Most of the country's people live in this central section, because conditions in the mountainous regions can be harsh in the winter months.

Opposite: **A mountain waterfall**

The Matterhorn

Alpine Legends

The Alps are among the most treacherous and challenging mountains in the world. During the mid-1800s, mountain climbing was a popular English hobby. Many climbers perished trying to conquer the infamous Matterhorn with its jagged and domineering peak. So many of these adventurers died that there is an entire cemetery in Zermatt for those who never made it. Finally, on July 14, 1865, an Englishman named Edward Whymper and his team became the first to reach the top. In 1904, the Alpine Museum was opened to honor that climb and many other brave deeds in the dangerous Alps.

Dinosaurs in the Alps?

More than 200 million years ago, the slopes of Mount San Giorgio in the Ticino canton were part of a seabed. During this time, which was called the Triassic Period, the dinosaurs first appeared, and land and water reptiles roamed the region. The fossil beds of the mountain show that reptiles once lived there. Some of these fossils can be seen in the Museum of Paleontology in Melide.

The Alpine Region

The Alps, which cover 60 percent of Switzerland, are the largest mountain system in Europe. They are named for their snow-capped peaks—the word *alp* comes from a Latin word meaning "white." The Alps extend beyond Switzerland, reaching to the east through Liechtenstein, Germany, Austria, and Slovenia. To the southwest, the Alps are part of the landscape in northern Italy and France.

The highest mountain in Switzerland is Mount Dufourspitze of Monte Rosa in the Alps. The highest mountain in the Alps, however, is Mont Blanc, which straddles France and Italy at 15,771 feet (4,807 meters). Other well-known Swiss Alps are the Matterhorn at 14,692 feet (4,478 m) and the Jungfrau at 13,642 feet (4,158 m). The average height for the Alps is 3,576 feet (1,090 m), with over 100 peaks at or near the altitude of 13,000 feet (3,962 m).

Dufour's Peak

General Guillaume-Henri Dufour (1787–1875) was a popular hero of the Swiss Civil War. After bringing the war to a quick close with the loss of only 150 lives, Dufour persuaded the Catholics and Protestants to compromise. This led to the Constitution of 1848. In addition to his military career, he was an important civil engineer whose construction works improved Geneva. He helped establish the Red Cross in 1863 and presided over the convention in 1864 that drew up the Geneva rules of warfare. The tallest peak in Switzerland was named Dufourspitze in his honor.

The Alps shaped Switzerland's transportation, industry, and lifestyle in many ways.

Glaciers helped form the Alps.

Frozen Rivers

Glaciers—slow-moving rivers if ice—cover more than 600 square miles (1,556 sq km) of land in Switzerland. The crevices of the Swiss Alps are huge sheets of ice. Glaciers like these helped form great mountain systems like the Alps, with the help of wind and rain. The ice moves so slowly along the mountains that tunnels have been carved

An ice cave

inside these glaciers so that people can walk through and see the eerie blue-green glow of glacial ice. One spot where the ice has been carved into tunnels and caves is at the top of Mount Titlis, about 22 miles (35 km) south of Lucerne.

Glaciers do more than sit on top of the mountains, however. Little by little the ice melts—it is only a tiny part of the glacier, but enough to send streams of water down the mountainsides. Glaciers are actually a major source of water for the lakes and streams of Switzerland.

During the last Ice Age, when this region lay beneath a sheet of ice, the moving glaciers scraped across the landscape. At Glacier Gardens, in Lucerne, you can still see the grooves cut in the solid rock as the glaciers moved over the area, carrying huge boulders along like pebbles. As the glaciers melted, waterfalls were created within them, carving out big holes in the land called potholes. The Glacial Gardens is up to 26 feet (8 m) across and 32 feet (10 m) deep.

Nature's Art

Tucked away in Lauterbrunnen, about 9 miles (15 km) south of Interlaken, is Trümmelbach Falls, a spiral waterfall. For many thousands of years, a glacier slowly melted away there, sending streams of water down inside the cracks in the mountainside. Over time, the water carved a tunnel through the rock, twisting and pushing its way down. That glacial river left huge twisting caverns in the rocks that stretch up the side of the mountain today. Visitors can walk along special pathways to see inside the spectacular formation where the glowing blue-green water reflects on the smooth carved surface of the rocks as it runs down through the crevice.

Underground Wonders

As glaciers melt, the water carves paths in the rock below, sometimes cutting out steep-sided gorges and underground caves, called karst caves. Switzerland has more than 3,000 known caves. Cave exploration began to be popular around the end of the 1800s, and thanks to avid spelunkers, or cave explorers, about a dozen caves known today are safe to explore.

The Hölloch cave in the Muotatal Valley of the Schwyz canton is the longest cave system in Europe. It is 93 miles (150 km) long, and 1/2 mile (0.8 km) of it is open to the public. With more than 100,000 tourists every year, it is the most visited cave in Switzerland. Tourists can travel by boat on its glacial waters, through the beautifully carved rocks. The largest underground lake in Europe is the St. Leonard. The water in this lake is always at a constant 51° Fahrenheit (11° Celsius) and is home to four kinds of trout. Legend says that if a young girl gazes into the surface of the lake, she will see her future husband's face gazing back!

At Baar Hölgrotten in Zug canton, huge conelike mineral deposits called stalactites (projecting down) and stalagmites (projecting up) cover the ceilings and floors of large caves. In some

The Fairy Grotto

Near St. Moritz in the Valais canton, an underground lake was discovered in 1863. Its tubelike tunnels lead to a 164-foot (50-m) waterfall inside the caves. Here also is the Fairy Fountain, where, according to legend, anyone who dips their hand in the fountain will get one wish granted.

Exploring one of Switzerland's many caves

places, the stalagmites rise so high that they meet the stalactites, creating immense pillars. The Bernese Oberland, above Lake Thun, has a cave believed to have been the home of Stone Age people. The cave was named Beatushöhlen after Saint Beatus who hid here in the sixth century.

From the Mountains to the Sea

The Rhine and the Rhone Rivers are both a result of glacial drainage. These two major rivers were "born" within 15 miles (24 km) of each other, near the St. Gotthard Pass. The mountains here divide the land like a ridge, so the Rhine flows

The Rhine River winding through the mountains

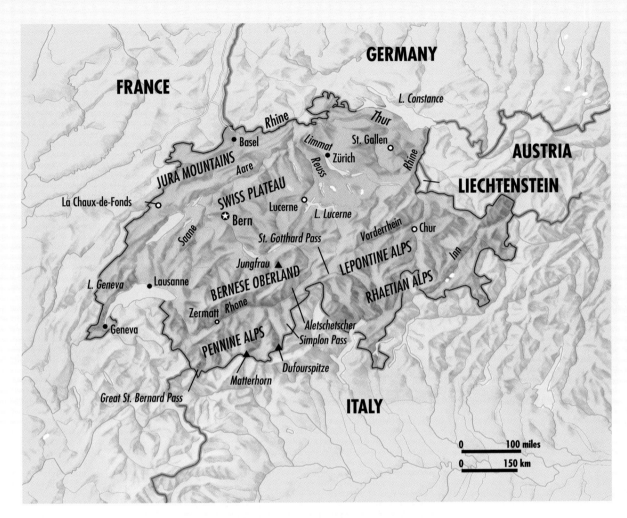

Switzerland's Geographical Features

Highest Elevation: Mount Dufourspitze of Monte Rosa, 15,203 feet (4,634 m) above sea level

Lowest Elevation: Lake Maggiore shoreline, 633 feet (193 m) above sea level

Longest River: Rhine, 233 miles (375 km) within Switzerland

Widest Lake: Lac Leman (Lake Geneva), 224 square miles (584 sq km)

Largest Glacier: Aletschgletscher, 14.6 miles (23 km) long

Largest City: Zürich

Location with Lowest Average Temperature: Peak of Mount Dufourspitze

Location with Highest Average Temperature: Ticino canton

Greatest Distance East–West: 213 miles (343 km)

Greatest Distance North–South: 138 miles (222 km)

The Rhone River near Sion

north to the North Sea, while the Rhone flows south to the Mediterranean. This line of division along the spine of the mountains is called a watershed line. Where the glacial runoff and rain or melted snow will end up depends on which side of the Alps it falls on. Water that does not flow north or south generally flows east off the Alps. The Ticino River, originating in the same region as the Rhine and the Rhone, eventually flows into the Po River, which flows east through Italy and empties into the Adriatic Sea. The Inn River, originating in a southeastern section, eventually flows into the Danube River, which reaches all the way to the Black Sea.

Pools of Turquoise

The lakes of Switzerland are fed by melting glaciers as well as by rain and groundwater. The blue-green water that comes from the glaciers can color an entire lake. Many lakes in Switzerland have this glowing quality, including Lake Lucerne, Lake Constance, and Lake Geneva.

Switzerland has 523 square miles (1,355 sq km) of inland water made up of more than 1,400 lakes. The lakes are used for recreation and transportation, prized for their fresh clean water, and appreciated for their natural beauty.

Mittelland

The central strip of gently rolling valleys that runs northeast to southwest through Switzerland is often referred to as the Swiss Plateau. The average altitude of the plateau is 1,700 feet (518 m), but it is much lower than the towering mountains around it. This area, which makes up only 30 percent of the

Farmland of the plateau

land, is home to four-fifths of the Swiss population. Here crops are grown, animals are raised, industry thrives, and people come to live.

Jurassic Mountains

The Jura Mountains run along Switzerland's western border. The Jura are almost parallel to the Alps, creating a sort of protective wall around the Swiss Plateau. The Jura Mountains cover about 10 percent of Switzerland's area, and reach an average height of 2,460 feet (750 m), about 1,000 feet (305 m) less than the average Alp height.

A hiker in the Jura Mountains

The Jura Mountains are much older than the Alps, and are named after the Jurassic Period which began about 208 million years ago. In the Celtic language, the word *jura* means "forest," and the term Jurassic Period comes from this word. Many fossils from that period have been found in the region. The highest mountain in the range is Mont Tendre, reaching up to 5,518 feet (1,682 m). This region is home to Switzerland's famous watchmaking industry and is also involved with lumber production and dairy farming.

Subzero to Sunny

The climate in Switzerland is as diverse as its people. At the tops of the Alps, freezing temperatures make the terrain dangerous and unlivable. But in the same tiny country, the warm Ticino region gets 58 percent of the possible hours of sunshine in each year.

As a rule, altitude influences climate. When the elevation increases 1,000 feet (300 m), the temperature drops 3° F (2° C). Higher elevations also get more precipitation, usually in the form of snow. Above 6,000 feet

The warm Ticino region

(1,800 m), snow falls for six months of the year. Precipitation in the highest peaks can reach 100 inches (250 centimeters) per year. Rochers de Naye, a mountain near Montreux, gets the most precipitation—about 102 inches (260 cm) per year.

In general, the western parts of Switzerland get more precipitation because of clouds coming in from the Atlantic coast. Clouds that move from the south are blocked by the Alps and lose their moisture.

Below the peaks, the sheltered valleys can become very hot in the summer. In the Swiss Plateau, temperatures average 60° to 70° F (16° to 21° C) in the summer, but the Ticino canton reaches an average high of 83° F (29° C), with much milder winters than any other canton. The warmer regions are at higher risk for severe storms, however, because dramatic temperature changes in such a small area tend to cause bad weather. The average yearly precipitation in the plateau is 40 to 45 inches (100 to 114 cm), and it can be much less in sheltered valleys.

The *foehn*, a warm wind that comes from the south, is one dangerous result of clashing temperatures. It comes in early spring, bringing with it not only hot air, but changes in air pressure. The foehn's warm air brings rain to the south of the Alps, but it can cause avalanches in the mountains when the snow melts too fast. Some people say the foehn causes headaches. However, the warm air also makes the mountains look much closer than they are, providing incredible views. In contrast to the foehn, a northeasterly breeze blows freezing temperatures across the valleys during the winter.

Looking at Switzerland's Cities

Basel

Basel was founded in the first century B.C. as a Roman stronghold, and the Augst ruins are still a landmark of the city. Other landmarks include the market square and an impressive cathedral. Today, Basel has a population of approximately 174,007. Standing at an elevation between 895 and 925 feet (273-282 m), the city enjoys cool temperatures in the summer, reaching as high as 74° F (24° C), and winter temperatures as low as 24° F (-4° C).

Geneva

Geneva's lakeside parks and gardens, warm summer temperatures, and the *Palais des Nations* (Palace of the Nations) makes it one of Switzerland's most visited cities. 173,559 people live there year round, and experience its winter lows of 29° F (-2° C). The city was founded under this name in 120 B.C. by Romans, who took over an old Celtic settlement. It stands at 1,227 feet (375 m) above sea level.

Lausanne

Taken over from successive Iron Age and Bronze Age settlers by the Romans in 47 B.C., Lausanne is now home to 115,878 people. The city's most impressive landmark is the cathedral, which is known as the finest Gothic building in Switzerland. The city enjoys July highs of 77° F (25° C) and January lows of 29° F (-2° C), and sits at an elevation of 1,493 feet (455 m) above sea level.

Zürich

Zürich's first settlers founded a community here around 4500 B.C. It became home to Celtic settlers a thousand years later. Zürich is home to the Swiss National Museum and beautiful gardens along the lake shore. The city's altitude is 1,339 feet (408 m) above sea level. Population today is 343,869 people, who enjoy the city's moderate year-round temperatures averaging 26° to 36° F (-3° to 2° C) in January and 56° to 76° F (14° to 25° C) in July.

Alpine Slopes and Tropical Palm Trees

S WITZERLAND'S UNIQUE GEOGRAPHY PROVIDES AN INTER-
esting combination of climates and habitats for its plants and
animals. The high, cold mountains are inhospitable to most
wildlife. One-fourth of Switzerland's land area is also able to
support only mosses and lichens. Fortunately, subtropical
plants can grow in some southern areas.

Opposite: **Roe deer in snow**

**Evergreen trees thrive at
higher elevations.**

Pines to Palms

Both evergreens and deciduous trees
grow in the forests of Switzerland. In
general, the hardier evergreens, such
as pine and fir trees thrive at high elevations, while leafy trees, such as
chestnut and beech, prefer lower alti-
tudes and warmer temperatures.

The Ticino canton, in the southern
part of Switzerland, has palm trees and
mimosas. Here, subtropical plants that
are native to the area grow on a penin-
sula called the Ceresio, surrounded by
the lake after which it is named.

Since Switzerland has few natural
resources, many of its trees were
harvested for lumber in the past.
The resulting deforestation problems

Alpine Slopes and Tropical Palm Trees   **27**

worried early environmentalists. In 1876, laws protecting the forests were passed, making them among the world's first environmental laws. These laws regulated the number of trees that could be cut and in what areas.

Preserving the Landscape

The Swiss Foundation for the Protection and Care of the Landscape, established in 1970, passed more strict regulations

Alpine flowers

on forest-cutting and other environmental issues. The laws protect rare or endangered plants, including the fragile Alpine edelweiss and the great blue thistle. With recent technology and more adventurous sport enthusiasts, new concerns have developed. Skiers are taking helicopters to previously undisturbed areas, tipping the delicate balance of Alpine ecology.

Along with establishing general protection agencies, the government has set aside large areas where the land is completely protected in its natural state. The first of these—Karpf Game Preserve—was an animal reserve set aside in 1548 in the canton of Glarus.

But one site in Switzerland has been saved by local people. Mount Generoso, a lovely spot in the far south of the warm Ticino canton, has been discussed as a

tourist site. Conflict arose between those who wanted to capitalize on the area's natural beauty by making it a tourist attraction with hotels, swimming pools, and golf courses, and those who wanted to preserve it for the people as one of the last spots of untouched nature. Ecologists, who are trying to keep the tourism industry from spoiling the area, have gathered support and are winning the battle.

The Swiss National Park was established in 1909 in the southern canton of Graubünden. This park consists of 40,690 acres (16,577 hectares) of preserved area where hunting, logging, and development are banned. The Riegelsee Wildlife Park, near Bern, is another preserve for animals. A number of botanical gardens and eight Alpine gardens are also protected. The most unusual garden is Brissago, on an island in Lake Maggiore, which Switzerland shares with Italy. Brissago was owned by a Russian countess who brought tropical plants from all over the world to this warm island. When the Swiss people heard that the island was about to be turned into a gambling casino, they took up a collection and bought it, protecting this tropical paradise forever.

Alpine Animals

The Alps provide a wonderful habitat for both the chamois and the ibex, which thrive in the Alpine climate and can be found throughout this region. They are not always welcomed by their human neighbors, however, since the hungry animals like to eat fresh vegetables from people's gardens. The chamois is a goatlike antelope and the ibex is a wild goat.

A chamois leaping across a mountain slope

The Bears of Bern

Bern's city pets are kept in a special open cage, close to the Nydegg Bridge. This round bear pit is so popular with locals and visitors that you will always find people there feeding the animals bread, carrots, and fruit. The bears show their appreciation by standing up and tumbling.

In Bern, it is a tradition for newlyweds to feed the bears on their wedding day. This custom began in medieval times, and the bears are celebrated in statues all over the city. They are also depicted on old coins and flags, as well as on every shopfront and on souvenirs. The bear also represents the Abbey of St. Gallen, and can be found on the shield of the canton of Appenzell.

Both animals have brown coats, but the chamois has more colorful markings that change with the season. The ibex has a small beard and massive horns up to 34 inches (85 cm) long. The chamois seems to defy the laws of gravity as it leaps from rock to rock on the steep slopes. Only a few hours after birth, a baby chamois can follow its mother on its tiny legs down impossibly steep slopes without skidding or falling.

A marmot enjoying the sun

The Alpine marmot is a relatively passive and shy resident of this area. In the lower regions of the Alps, the predatory lynx is seldom seen by humans. The lynx has a light-brown coat with dark spots and a dark tip at the end of its tail. Its paws are large, with a thick padding of fur. The lynx rarely grows larger than 64 pounds (29 kilograms). It lives in forests and eats rodents.

Deer run free in southeastern Switzerland. The roe deer, which lives in the forest and at woodland edges, changes its color with the seasons. In summer, it is a reddish brown with a grey face, and in winter it blends into the snowy landscape with a grayish coat and white patches at its throat.

The Brave Saint Bernards

The Saint Bernard is a large, intelligent dog known for rescuing lost travelers. The dog was named for the snowy, dangerous mountain pass they traveled with the Saint Bernard monks who were responsible for keeping the Alpine pass open in the winter. The size of these dogs was especially useful for pushing snow out of the way to clear a path for travelers, and their keen senses kept everyone safely on course during the worst snowstorms or in the thickest fogs. Saint Bernards were used as regular guides by 1750 and saved more than 2,000 people over the next 150 years.

The dogs in the St. Bernard Pass were very successful as rescue dogs. These brave animals were always able to find travelers lost in a blizzard. With their help, Napoléon's entire army of 250,000 men were able to cross the pass safely. Not a single person was lost during that march. The most famous Saint Bernard, named Barry, helped rescue more than 40 people. Today, his stuffed body is on exhibit in the Natural History Museum in Bern.

Saint Bernards have worked as guide and rescue dogs.

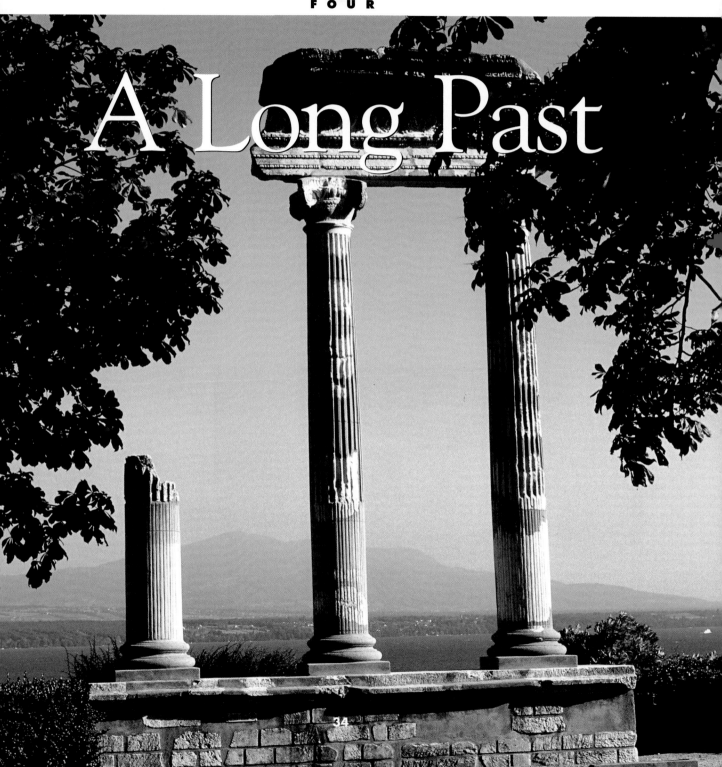

A Long Past

I N ORDER TO UNDERSTAND SWITZERLAND'S VARIED PEOPLE, it helps to know something about its history. Its cultural diversity is a result of many different groups coming together to preserve and defend a special way of life.

Opposite: **Roman ruins at Nyon on Lake Geneva**

The First Settlers

About 50,000 years ago, groups of Stone Age people lived in caves in the mountains of what is now Switzerland. Their artifacts have been found in caves in the Bernese Oberland, and other evidence has been found in Ebenalp, in the canton of Appenzell, and in Schweizerbild, in the canton of Schaffhausen. The first people to settle in the area probably enjoyed the safety of higher, more sheltered areas. This protection, combined with a fresh water source, made mountainous lakesides ideal for early people.

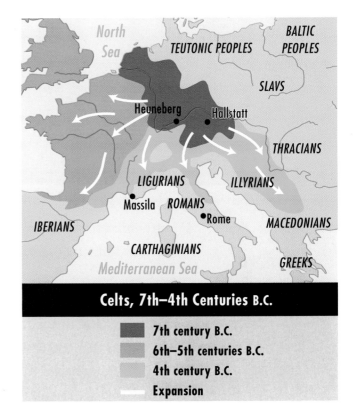

Celts, 7th–4th Centuries B.C.

- 7th century B.C.
- 6th–5th centuries B.C.
- 4th century B.C.
- Expansion

The Helvetti and Rhaeti Move In

As time went on, the number of tiny villages grew, and tribes from other areas soon began moving into the land. People

The Helvetti planning their migration

called the Helvetti, a Celtic tribe traveling across the continent, settled there before 500 B.C. Another group called the Rhaeti, who came north from what is now Italy, settled alongside the Helvetti in mountain passes, although not peacefully.

After some time, groups of invaders from the north, mostly Germanic tribes, began to move into Helvetti territory. Unwilling to fight the constant raids, they moved away. In 58 B.C., large numbers of Helvetti packed what they could carry, rounded up their livestock, and headed west to find a new place to live. The group traveled toward a spot on the mouth of the Garonne River on the Atlantic coast.

Romans Take Charge

When Roman leader Julius Caesar heard about the bands of refugees moving toward land that he controlled, he put a stop to it. He ordered his army to make the 700-mile (1,126-km) trip as fast as they could. After only eight days, the army reached Geneva. The Roman soldiers stopped the Helvetti near present-day Autun. Caesar demanded that the Helvetti return to the Alps, and sent his soldiers to make sure they stayed there.

Julius Caesar

By sending thousands of troops back to the Alps with the defeated Helvetti, Caesar gained control over the area. Although the groups of Helvetti and Rhaeti were under Roman law, they enjoyed some benefits. The Romans not only threw out the Germanic tribes, but also introduced new foods, such as cherries and chicken. They helped to improve the breeds of cattle that grazed in the Alps and taught the Helvetti how to develop better vineyards.

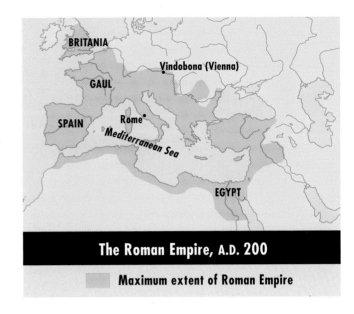

The Roman Empire, A.D. 200

Maximum extent of Roman Empire

One of the most important contributions the Romans made, however, was their experience in building a community—the basics of government, transportation, and commerce. The Romans helped develop the St. Bernard Pass, which connected Italy to northern Europe. Much of their help was in their own interests, of course. Now Romans controlled the best passage between their territory and northern Europe.

The St. Bernard Pass today

The Romans also established a legal system, imposing Roman law and Roman governors. In addition, they also built amphitheaters, some of which are still used today.

After the Legions Left

In the A.D. 400s, after hundreds of years of occupation, the Roman soldiers went home to defend their own land. With no major army to stop them, two groups from surrounding areas began to move in and take over. Burgundians swept through from the west, while the Alemanni came in from the north. The two groups met—and stopped—at the Sarine River, which thus became the border between the French-speaking and German-speaking sections, as it is today.

Power Struggles

Although the Romans had physically left the region, it was still considered their territory. The Frankish emperor Charlemagne took control of their lands, which became part of the Holy

Charlemagne dressed for battle

Roman Empire in A.D. 962. All the rest of what is now Switzerland was included in the empire by 1033.

After Charlemagne's death in 814, the land was divided and given to two of his grandsons. In the confusion that resulted, the Holy Roman Empire's power decreased. Soon, strong local families began to rule in their own regions.

Feudal Switzerland

Like much of Europe during these centuries, the Swiss land was ruled by bishops and ducal families, who taxed and ruled their fiefs—the land they owned—independently in a feudal system. All of these independent fiefs were loosely under the leadership of the Holy Roman Empire.

Carolingian Empires

Kingdom of the Franks, 768

Farthest extent of Charlemagne's empire

Partition of Verdun, 843

The Rise of the Habsburgs

After the territory was split apart, the lack of unity and organization took its toll on the people. Law and order was lost in some areas, and the wealthy families began to form their own armies, taking over sections of the country. Two powerful families, the Savoie of France and the Habsburgs of Austria, eventually dominated.

As time passed, the Habsburg influence grew and soon the family controlled most of the Holy Roman Empire. Under

Four Languages in One Tiny Country

With Roman armies no longer there to protect it, the northern and eastern areas were invaded by troops from Germany, while French armies moved in from the west. The line where their battles stopped is still the border between French-speaking and German-speaking Switzerland.

South of the forbidding mountains of the Alps, beyond the reach of these armies, people still spoke Latin. In one region, the Latin evolved into a language called Romansh. Today, Romansh is spoken only in remote areas of Ticino canton by a very small percentage of the population. Most Ticino people speak Italian.

Rudolf of Habsburg

Count Rudolf of Habsburg, district governors—mostly Habsburgs—were appointed. They angered local leaders and citizens by their harsh rule and high taxes. To make things worse, trade declined and crops failed, which made it even harder for people to pay the high taxes demanded by the Habsburgs. During these trying times, the story of William Tell arose. Whether it was based in fact or legend, it inspired the downtrodden peasants who were struggling for freedom.

The Eternal Pact

People in the Uri, Schwyz, and Unterwalden regions became frustrated with the way their affairs were being run from so far away. They realized that they could govern themselves much better since they were more in touch with the needs of their people. Leaders from these three states met secretly in Rütli on Lake Lucerne and declared their alliance and self-government by signing the Perpetual Covenant. This agreement, signed on August 1, 1291, was the beginning of the Swiss Confederation, which still exists today. August 1 is celebrated as Swiss Independence Day. The original document, written

William Tell—Man or Myth?

No one really knows whether a man named William Tell ever lived or whether anyone ever shot an apple off his son's head. But real or not, William—Wilhelm in German—Tell lives in the hearts of the Swiss. Each summer, in Altdorf, his life story is performed on an outdoor stage, not so much for tourists as for local people who have enjoyed the play for generations.

The story begins in the troubled years when Switzerland was controlled by the Holy Roman Empire and oppressed by a tyrannical governor named Gessler. His subjects were ordered to remove their hats as they passed Gessler's hat nailed to a post. When William Tell refused, he was arrested, and sent to prison. An expert archer, he bargained that if he could shoot an apple off the top of his son's head, he would be freed. Of course he succeeded, or there would be no story of William Tell to tell.

Instead of walking away a free man, however, he turned and shot a second arrow through Gessler's hat. He was arrested again, but he escaped from a boat on his way to prison by jumping to a rock on the shore. He then became an outlaw leader in the Swiss fight against oppression. In this role, with his unerring marksmanship, he later killed Gessler.

Along with the play, Tell is remembered by a museum in Bürglen, his supposed birthplace. At the rock where he escaped from his captors, a chapel has been built in his honor. The Schiller Stone, a large natural obelisk in the water, is dedicated to Schiller, the man who wrote the play of Tell's life: "To him who sang Tell's glory."

Saving the Rütli

To the Swiss people, the meadow of Rütli, where the Perpetual Covenant of the three original cantons was signed, is a symbol of freedom and peace. In 1940, General Guisan chose this spot to declare Swiss national unity to the world. This meadow is still cherished by the Swiss—but it was almost lost to Switzerland forever.

At one point, the land where such important events in Switzerland's history had taken place was up for sale, and developers had other plans for it. Concerned schoolchildren across the country decided to protest. The children raised enough money to buy the land and keep it from being sold to someone who would change it forever. It is still owned by the schoolchildren of Switzerland.

in Latin, is exhibited in Schwyz, the town for which the country was named. Rütli is still Switzerland's most patriotic site.

The Habsburgs did not take this lying down, and the Swiss had to defend their new Confederation against an army ten times as strong as their own. In 1315, at Morgarten, an army of peasants defeated the Austrian Habsburg army. Their success encouraged five more cantons to join the original three, increasing the manpower of the rebel army. These courageous cantons were Lucerne, Zürich, Bern, Glarus, and Zug. The

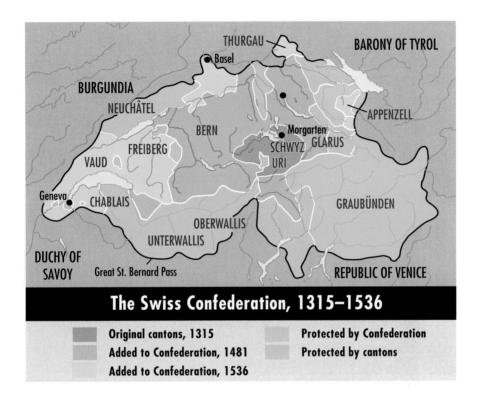

The Swiss Confederation, 1315–1536

Original cantons, 1315
Added to Confederation, 1481
Added to Confederation, 1536

Protected by Confederation
Protected by cantons

added troops enabled the Swiss, now finally a united people, to again defeat the Austrian army in 1386 at Sempach and in 1388 at Näfels.

The Swiss Army Becomes Famous

By the 1400s, the Swiss were gaining a reputation throughout Europe as a strong military power. Patriotism was high and many young men chose the army as an alternative to struggling through the tough economic problems of the time. Because of this, the army grew rapidly, and Switzerland began expanding its land through occupation. Burgundy, in what is now France, was an independent kingdom that still occupied

Independence from the Holy Roman Empire, 1648

Swiss Confederation, 1486
Added to Confederation by 1500
Added to Confederation by 1648

Temporarily held by
the Confederation
Borders of the Holy
Roman Empire

territories west of the Confederated cantons. The Swiss army defeated Charles the Bold of Burgundy in 1477, gaining the large territory north and east of Lake Geneva.

Despite these successes, the Swiss were still struggling to gain their independence from the Habsburgs' Holy Roman Empire. In 1476, and again in 1499, the Swiss defeated Habsburg forces, but it wasn't until 1648 that the Holy Roman Empire officially recognized Switzerland's independence.

Switzerland Grows

After the Swiss had defeated both the French and the Habsburgs, small neighboring regions began to respect them, realizing the strength in numbers. Many small areas asked to join the Confederation, but the original cantons were not always anxious to have them. In fact, they argued among themselves over each new addition, and almost went to war with one another over the admittance of new states.

Finally, a farmer named Nicholas of Flue persuaded the canton leaders to compromise instead of fighting. He helped the cantons of Fribourg and Solothurn join the Confederation in 1481. Basel and Schaffhausen followed in 1501, then Appenzell in 1513. Nicholas's calm, wise influence was so important to the Swiss that in 1947 he was made patron saint of Switzerland. He set an example of compromise in the face of argument that resulted in an entirely new vision for his country, an idea almost unknown in Europe during these troubled times.

From this time forward, instead of becoming involved in all the petty squabbles of neighboring countries, Switzerland remained neutral. Along with this policy came the realization that the nation could not remain neutral and still expand its borders forcefully. The famous Swiss army then concerned itself only with protecting—not with expanding. This philosophy has continued to guide Switzerland through the centuries. However, this did not prevent the Swiss from hiring themselves out as professional soldiers. These "soldiers for hire" are known as mercenaries.

Swiss mercenaries fought in other people's wars. Swiss troops even fought during the American Civil War and served as bodyguards for Francis I, a French king during the 1500s. Even today, a group of paid Swiss soldiers stand proudly in front

A Swiss soldier standing guard at Vatican City

of Vatican City, guarding the home of the Roman Catholic Church and serving as personal guards to the pope. They have been protecting the pope in Rome for nearly 500 years.

Finally, in 1874, the Swiss Constitution banned other countries from buying the services of the Swiss soldiers. However, this law did not prevent soldiers from volunteering for other armies. The right to volunteer was finally taken away in 1927, with one exception—the Swiss Guards at the Vatican.

The Lion of Lucerne

During the French Revolution, Europe was in turmoil. As mercenaries, Swiss soldiers fought against the revolutionaries in France. Their job was to protect the royalty and government of France from the violence and rioting of the citizens. In 1792, an angry mob stormed the Tuileries Palace in Paris, which the Swiss were guarding. More than 700 Swiss mercenaries died in that uprising.

In memory of this heroic event in which Swiss lives were lost to save others, Danish sculptor Bertel Thorvaldsen carved a monument to their bravery and sacrifice. The Lion of Lucerne is an enormous statue carved on a rock. Leaning on his sword and shield, the lion is dying. He sits in a cave, which has been carved out behind him. This monument is near the

Glacier Garden in Lucerne, forever part of the landscape as a constant reminder of the pain of war.

Religious Conflicts

During the middle of the sixteenth century, the Swiss had many struggles over religion. Switzerland's mixed religious background was a result of the varied cultures in the country and ranged from Catholic to German pagan influences. Prior to these times, the various religions had coexisted without too much trouble, but many people began to take sides in the new debates, and it became harder to keep the peace. One of the biggest movements of the time focused on removing corruption from the Roman Catholic Church, a crusade led by a man named Ulrich Zwingli.

Like Zwingli, many priests were opposed to the Catholic Church's practices. Unfortunately, even though they were working against the same corruption, they disagreed among themselves.

Soon, another reformer, named John Calvin, came on the scene. He wanted to make church doctrines even stricter. A Protestant, his influence formed the ideals for the Puritans. This superstrict way did not suit everyone, but Calvin's influence spread all over Europe from his base in Geneva.

Unfortunately, the religious arguments led to a great deal of violence. Many battles were fought over religious concerns and for religious control. While these internal fights were going on, Switzerland stayed out of the troubles plaguing the rest of Europe. The Thirty Years' War was dragging on in a constant struggle over land and religion. At the end of this war, a pact called the Treaty of Westphalia brought peace to the continent. In this pact, Switzerland's neutrality was recognized by the other European countries.

Revolution in France

The rebellion of the American colonists and their defeat of the British swept a fever for freedom through Europe. In 1789, French peasants, tired of unfair rule, launched the bloody French Revolution. The heat of the revolution reached neighboring Switzerland with the arrival of French troops. They quickly occupied the country and set up the Helvetic Republic—under the control of the French. This was formed in 1798, but by 1803 the cantons were once again part of the Confederation.

Switzerland's reunification was a result of Napoléon Bonaparte, the leader of France after the revolution. Unity did not come without a price, however. Napoléon used

Napoléon crossing the Alps

Switzerland as a battlefield in his wars against the Austrians, Prussians, and Russians. Meanwhile, the Swiss themselves were in a state of disorder. Napoléon took this opportunity to impose his Act of Mediation in 1803. This law recognized the

Swiss Federation and the equality of the cantons and the local communities. Napoléon also added six new cantons, Aargau, St. Gallen, Graubünden, Thurgau, Ticino, and Vaud, somewhat neutralizing the power that the German cantons had held as a majority.

Learning to Get Along

When Napoléon was finally defeated in his attempts to overrun Europe, the Congress of Vienna recognized the Swiss Confederation as an independent country with both its original boundaries and its new cantons. This international agreement also recognized Switzerland's neutrality, which it has maintained to this day. The Congress of Vienna did not solve all of Switzerland's problems, however. The government still had to figure out a way for all the cantons, with varying geography, different religions, changing economies, and different customs, to work together as a single country. Some people, especially the powerful aristocrats, wanted to keep the old ways. Others, inspired by the changes occurring in other countries in Europe began to form a strong liberal movement. Several cantons removed their old aristocratic families from power and developed forms of self-government by the lower classes.

The Catholic cantons were among the staunchest conservatives, but as they resisted change, they began to feel threatened by the growing popularity of the liberal movement. These Catholic cantons of central Switzerland made a pact to separate from the other cantons, forming a union known as the Sonderbund.

The Swiss Diet, a legislative body representing all the other cantons, met in Bern and voted to regain the Sonderbund. They sent an army, led by General Guillaume-Henri Dufour, to enforce their decision. Dufour was able to stop this uprising quickly and efficiently, without leaving the usual political debris. His campaign took only one month, with a loss of 150 soldiers. His swift action left the way open for a quick reconciliation with the Catholic cantons. But unrest continued as the Swiss struggled to find a balance with the federal power of the Confederation, religious freedom, and individual rights.

The growing unrest climaxed in 1845, in the midst of a terrible economic crisis. All across Europe, the staple crop of the lower classes—the potato—suffered a devastating crop failure. Famine raged from Ireland to the Alps. In addition, rising prices caused a depression in the textile industry, which was the chief occupation of many rural people. At this point, everyone realized that they must work together or starve separately.

The Swiss Adopt a Constitution

In 1848, representatives from all the cantons and towns met in Brunnen and in Treib to hammer out the details of a federal Constitution. It guaranteed a wide range of civil liberties. People could now live wherever they wanted to, meet freely, and be treated equally under the law. The attention paid to minority groups in this new Constitution proved that the Swiss had indeed learned from their eighteen years of bitter conflict. Local canton governments still had great powers in determining their own ways of life, as they do today.

The Red Cross

During 1859, when there was a war in Italy, a Swiss man named Jean Henri Dunant (photo) passed by the battlefield at Solferino the day after a major battle. As he looked out across the 40,000 dying and critically injured men, Dunant resolved that something had to be done for those who were suffering. Gathering volunteers, he formed a group to help the wounded soldiers. In 1862, Dunant published a moving account of what he saw, *Un Souvenir de Solferino (Recollections of Solferino)*. He ended the book with a plea: "Would it not be possible to found and organize in all civilized countries permanent societies of volunteers who in time of war would give help to the wounded without regard for their nationality?" Dunant shared the first Nobel Peace Prize in 1901.

This plea stirred the hearts of many. Representatives from sixteen nations and many other organizations from across the world came together and considered the possibility of a society of volunteers. Their first meeting was held on October 26, 1863, in Geneva. At this gathering, the symbol of a red cross on a white flag, the opposite of the Swiss flag, was chosen in honor of the heritage of the man who had conceived the idea. The basic plans for the organization were also set up, and in August 1864, the first official Geneva Convention took place. This convention also established the rules of warfare that are still observed today.

In the modern world, the Red Cross is a widespread organization that helps victims of war, poverty, and natural disaster. The Red Cross is also committed to education, especially concerning disease control, nutrition, and general health issues. Except for Muslim nations which chose a red crescent symbol on a white flag, Red Cross organizations around the world still use the flag originally chosen in 1863.

The results were astonishing. In only two years, the Swiss Confederation was recognized by the rest of Europe as second only to Great Britain as an industrialized nation. Interestingly, neither the Catholic conservatives, nor the old aristocrats challenged the new system. It was the intellectuals and lower classes that brought about the first significant change in the Constitution in 1869. After that, the government was elected directly by the people, and all bills in parliament had to be approved by a popular vote. The new Constitution of 1874 was the result of these pressures.

Protecting Prosperity

The new Constitution paved the way for Switzerland to focus on developing its economy. Farmers joined together in cooperatives to take advantage of the new rail transportation to export cheese, condensed milk, and chocolate. As the textile industry declined, the chemical and machine-building industries developed. Despite a lack of mineral, coal, or other raw materials, Switzerland was able to become a major player in international export.

Many Swiss rail lines were built in the nineteenth century.

The Alps played a large role in this. These high mountains running through the center of Europe made trade difficult between countries in the north and the south. In 1880, with some financial help from Germany and France, Swiss engineers cut a 9 1/2-mile (15-km) tunnel through the St. Gotthard Pass. Rail lines soon spread throughout Switzerland. In twenty years, 780 miles (1,255 km) of track were laid, and this figure more than doubled by 1885. Switzerland became the transportation center of Europe.

Europe Goes to War

Although the warring nations generally respected Switzerland's neutrality during World War I (1914–1918), it was severely tested at home. German-speaking Switzerland was pro-Germany, and some residents there passed secret military information across the border into Germany. But neutrality won out, and Swiss industry thrived as war raged all around its borders.

Unfortunately, the shortage of food brought on by war more than doubled food prices for the Swiss. A general strike by workers was quickly ended to the benefit of laborers, which secured a 48-hour workweek, an extended social security system, and the right to bargain as a group with their employers.

After World War I, the League of Nations was formed at an international peace conference in Paris. At this time, Switzerland also agreed to protect its tiny neighbor Liechtenstein with its army, enforce its customs regulations, and handle its diplomatic dealings with other countries. Between World Wars I and II, the Swiss economy slowly began shifting from manufacturing toward services. But in the meantime, Europe was moving toward war once again.

Surrounded by War Again

World War II (1939–1945) put an even heavier pressure on Switzerland's neutrality. When France was taken over by Hitler's armies in 1940, it left Switzerland completely surrounded by the Axis powers—Germany, Italy, and Austria. The Axis was a group of countries that supported Hitler's goal of dominating

During World War II, Adolph Hitler's Nazi regime criticized Switzerland's multicultural pride.

Europe. Even within Switzerland, many leading politicians felt that it would be wiser to work with the Germans than to risk being invaded.

But Switzerland had one advantage that protected them from the Nazis. Hitler feared that any attack on Switzerland would cause the Swiss to blow up the tunnels and passes through the Alps. In fact, the Swiss remained ready to do this throughout the war. Without the tunnels, now protected by Swiss neutrality, the Alps would once again divide the north and south. Since they were neutral, the Swiss posed no threat to the Nazis, and Hitler knew that if he won the war and controlled all of Europe, the Alps would be his for the taking.

Neutral Powers in World War II, 1939–45

Axis (German) ally
Occupied by Germany
Neutral power
Allied power

Throughout the war, Hitler's regime was openly critical of the multicultural pride of the Swiss, which was completely opposed to the Nazi racist philosophy. Switzerland took in 100,000 refugees and provided a base for international humanitarian groups, such as the Red Cross, during the long years of war.

Working for Peace

In 1945, at the end of World War II, the United Nations (UN) was formed in Geneva to replace the ineffective League of Nations. Although Switzerland hosted the meetings, it

Neutral or Not?

In 1997, the whole world was shocked to learn that the Swiss National Bank was still holding gold and other valuables the Nazis had taken from the countries they occupied during World War II. When the war ended, very little effort was made to return the assets to their rightful owners, or their heirs. The Swiss government, obviously upset by this embarrassing news, responded by requiring all the banks involved to release the records of these transactions. On August 12, 1998, a settlement of U.S.$1.25 billion was finally reached. This money is supposed to go to anyone who can prove it is theirs, or that they are the heir to the money. All money left over will be divided among Holocaust survivors everywhere.

chose not to join the UN because of the membership requirement to contribute armed forces to world peacekeeping, which would compromise Swiss neutrality.

Although Switzerland does not take part in such political organizations, it has been active in other European affairs. It helped create the European Free Trade Association in 1960, and was part of the 1963 Council of Europe, which worked for social and economic progress.

Women Get the Vote

Switzerland, for all its liberalism and concern for personal freedoms, was the last major European country to allow women to vote. In 1958, Basel became the first Swiss city to give women the vote in local elections. In 1971, women gained the right to vote in national elections, and ten years later, an equal rights amendment was approved by Swiss voters. But conservative areas, like the Appenzell canton, did not allow women to vote until 1991, twenty years after the amendment was adopted. It took yet another decade for women to work their way up to government positions.

Modern Switzerland

In 1979, another canton was born in Switzerland. No new land was added, but an existing canton was split in two. The capital city of Bern was divided from the rest of the canton, much as Washington, D.C. is, in the United States. This gave the administrative capital its own district, and made the total number of cantons 26.

Switzerland made news in 1999 when Swiss scientist Bertrand Piccard and his British copilot Brian Jones were the first people ever to go all the way around the world, nonstop in a hot-air balloon. They did not even stop to refuel.

Although Switzerland has no space program of its own, Swiss scientists take an active part in experiments and research. The shuttle *Discovery*, launched in 1998, carried an alpha magnetic spectrometer. This Swiss device is designed to detect antimatter particles in space and will return to space in 2002 to spend three to five years at the international space station.

The country is still a center for humanitarian work and peacekeeping, and when war broke out in Serbia's Kosovo province, they were among the first to send supplies to the suffering people there. Along with setting up refugee camps in Albania, Macedonia, and Montenegro, the Swiss have provided more than 470 tons (426,375 kg) of food and medicines and 670 tons (607,810 kg) of milk. Switzerland has welcomed 50,000 temporary refugees, about half the number they admitted during all of World War II.

Swiss scientist Bertrand Piccard (right) and Brian Jones in the gondola of their hot-air balloon

A Swiss aid shipment for Albanian refugees from Kosovo

The Fine Art of Compromise

CURIA CONFŒDERATIONIS HELVETICAE

S WITZERLAND'S GOVERNMENT IS CLASSIFIED AS A FEDERAL republic. Switzerland's administrative divisions include a federal government, cantonal government, district government, and municipalities. This system could be compared to the U.S. or Canadian system of federal government, state, county, and city or town government. But many of the similarities end here.

Switzerland's federal government is divided into three branches—legislative, executive, and judicial. The federal government is in charge of national issues, such as national security and the army. Most federal offices are in Bern, the administrative capital of Switzerland, where government business generally takes place.

Opposite: **The Federal Assembly building**

The Citizens' Army

The Swiss army is a unique institution, considering the country's neutrality and general antiviolence stand. However, Switzerland must have a strong military force for defense in case of attack. Service in the Swiss militia is required of all male citizens, who begin training at the age of twenty. After this, until a man reaches fifty, he must drop everything and serve if called. If health or work prevents it, a man may get out of serving in the army, but he must pay a special tax. At present, the Swiss army has 27,300 men.

The Swiss National Anthem

"Schweizer Psalm" ("Swiss Psalm"), Switzerland's national anthem, was composed by Albert Zwyssig (1808–1854).

When the morning skies grow red
And over us their radiance shed
Thou, O Lord, appeareth in their light
When the Alps glow bright with splendor,
Pray to God, to Him surrender
For you feel and understand
That He dwelleth in this land
For you feel and understand
That He dwelleth in this land

In the sunset thou art nigh
And beyond the starry sky

Thou, O loving father, ever near,
When to Heaven we are departing
Joy and bliss thou'lt be imparting
For we feel and understand
That thou dwellest in this land

When dark clouds enshroud the hills
And gray mist the valley fills
Yet thou art not hidden from thy sons
Pierce the gloom in which we cower
With thy sunshine's cleansing power
Then we'll feel and understand
That God dwelleth in this land
Then we'll feel and understand
That God dwelleth in this land

The federal government is also in charge of diplomatic relations with other countries. The nation's communications system is run by the government, as are the trains and customs regulations. However, several radio stations are privately owned. Other responsibilities include law enforcement and upholding the constitutions of the cantons. The federal government acts as a mediator in internal conflicts. The currency is also issued by the federal government.

The Legislative Branch

Switzerland's legislative branch is the Federal Assembly. In German, it is the *Bundesversammlung*; in French, the *Assemblée Fédérale*; and in Italian, the *Assemblea Federale*.

It is made up of two houses, the Council of States and the National Council.

The Council of States has forty-six members. Each of the twenty full cantons sends two representatives, and each of the six half-cantons sends one representative. They are chosen by the canton legislature or by a vote of the citizens, depending on the canton. Terms for this office run from one to four years.

The Council of States in session

Cooperation in Politics

Switzerland has many political parties, but three dominate the scene. These are the Christian Democratic Party, the Radical Democratic Party, and the Social Democratic Party. In many places, words like *radical* make us think of groups that take extreme measures and are unwilling to see other points of view. In Switzerland, however, there is a great deal of cooperation between the parties. They are required by law to have equal representation in the federal government, and the parties try to see eye to eye for the benefit of everyone. They feel that arguing for a particular opinion is not the best path to a solution.

The National Council has 200 members. The number of representatives from each canton is determined by its population, but each canton gets at least one representative. The terms for representatives are four years, and voters in the cantons choose their own representatives.

These two councils decide on army matters, and are also responsible for electing the president, vice president, federal chancellor, and members of the federal court and the military court of appeal.

A Symbol of Faith and Patriotism

The Swiss flag, like the country's name, originated in the canton of Schwyz. During the reign of Rudolf I of the Habsburg Empire, soldiers from this canton fought in his battles. They asked the king to let them place a white cross on their blood-red flags of war and, after their victory, he allowed them to use it. This symbol was later used by the three founding cantons as a battle banner. Today, the white cross stands for the nation's Christian values.

The Executive Branch

The Federal Council is the executive branch of the government. It consists of seven members. The president, elected by a group from the two legislative chambers, serves a one-year term and cannot be elected two years in a row. Each member of the executive branch heads a specific department, much like the U.S. Cabinet. The seven departments are foreign affairs, military, finance, justice and police, economy, transportation and energy, and internal affairs. One canton may not be represented by more than one member, and each political party is represented.

The seven members of the Federal Council for 2000

The National Justice Building

The Judicial Branch

The federal court is the final judicial authority, which means that its rulings are indisputable. The federal court is made up of twenty-six judges elected by the Federal Assembly. Their powers include overruling cantonal court decisions, but they may not veto laws passed by the Federal Assembly.

NATIONAL GOVERNMENT OF SWITZERLAND

FEDERAL ASSEMBLY

COUNCIL OF STATES   NATIONAL COUNCIL

PRESIDENT   FEDERAL COURT

FEDERAL COUNCIL

Bern: Did You Know This?

The city of Bern became Switzerland's capital in 1848. The old town features landmarks such as a colorful street known as the Marktgasse. In Bern you will also find the Clock Tower, the Bear Pit, and a Gothic cathedral built in the fifteenth century.

Population: 127,469

Year founded: 1191 by Duke Berchtold of Zaringen

Altitude: 1,772 feet (540 m)

Average daily temperature: 24° to 34° F (−4° to 1° C) in January; 54° to 74° F (13° to 24° C) in July

Average annual rainfall: 42.9 inches (109 cm) with more than 5 inches (13 cm) a month usually falling in June and July

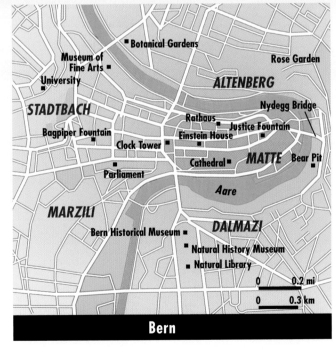

An Indirect Democracy

The system of appointing the executive branch by a vote of the legislative branch makes Switzerland an indirect democracy. This does not mean that the people have no say in what goes on, however. The citizens of Switzerland can make a direct impact on their government in two ways.

If 100,000 citizens sign a petition, they can call for a vote concerning a change or addition to the constitution or to the federal laws. This is called an Initiative. Also, citizens can directly influence the government through a referendum. A referendum can be raised by 50,000 citizens when the executive branch wants to pass a law or change the Constitution. Through a referendum, citizens can override the decision of the executive branch.

The Swiss may call for ten to fifteen of these special votes a year. Clearly, when added with local, cantonal, and national elections, the Swiss spend a lot of time going to the polls to vote. The voting age is 18. Voter turnout in Switzerland is among the highest in the world, and the Swiss are well-informed about each issue. Perhaps this is because of the hundreds of newspapers available for them to read.

Governing the Cantons

One major aspect of Swiss government is the power of the cantons. In order to have unity and protection, the cantons wanted a common bond and constitution, but they did not want to lose their individuality. Because the unique qualities and conditions of each canton are most easily understood by those who live there, a great deal of power remains with the individual cantons. There are twenty full cantons in Switzerland, plus an additional six half-cantons. This makes the official number twenty-three cantons, even though there are twenty-six different names. The cantonal government is set up like the federal government, but each canton runs things differently.

Cantonal governments are responsible for certain specific areas. Their specific rules and duties, detailed in the canton's constitution, include decisions about education, local transportation—especially, the roads— and social institutions.

Cantons

1	Aargau	10	Graubünden	19	Soleure
2	Appenzell, Outer	11	Jura	20	Thurgau
3	Appenzell, Inner	12	Lucerne	21	Ticino
4	Baselland	13	Neuchâtel	22	Uri
5	Baselstadt	14	Nidwalden	23	Valais
6	Bern	15	Obwalden	24	Vaud
7	Fribourg	16	St. Gallen	25	Zug
8	Geneva	17	Schaffhausen	26	Zürich
9	Glarus	18	Schwyz		

Raise Your Hand

In today's world of electronic polls and complicated anonymous voting systems, it is nice to know that somewhere the vote of a single raised hand still counts. Switzerland's traditional open-air voting system, called *landsgemeinden*, is held in town squares in the cantons of Appenzell, Glarus, and Unterwalden. Votes are taken by a count of raised hands. This old style of voting is prized as an important part of the Swiss way of life.

Swiss Citizenship

Each native-born Swiss is registered with the federal government and considered a Swiss citizen. People may also become Swiss by marriage, or by naturalization with a vote by citizens. But to the Swiss, citizenship is more than a vague allegiance. Besides federal citizenship, a Swiss person has cantonal and communal citizenship. Each person is registered with the canton as a citizen with certain rights within that canton.

The community citizenship is a unique aspect of Swiss life. Community citizenship is required, as is registry with federal and cantonal governments. It carries a responsibility to other community members, and this is where the family records are kept. The interesting thing is that a person's community citizenship is not necessarily the place where they are born, or even the canton of their citizenship. It is a family community. Even when later generations move to other areas and have children there, they are still considered part of the original family community.

This community is responsible for providing financial help to citizens in need, and finding a home for the elderly citizens. More modern systems in some regions take care of all those who live in the community, even non-citizens. In past centuries, many Swiss communities "helped" their poor citizens by buying an overseas passage to get rid of the burden.

Local Government

Bezirke are districts, much like counties in the United States and Canada. The executive branch of the district makes decisions about local laws. The districts are responsible for education and most legal issues. They administer the basic court systems that are used day to day.

Municipalities

The *Gemeinden* are municipalities, including town and city governments. There are 3,029 municipalities, also known as communes. Municipalities with fewer than 10,000 citizens are called villages. Those with larger populations are called towns.

The voting citizens are considered the legislative power in the municipalities. Executive decisions are made by the town council or the village council. The judicial branch of the

Towns and villages are responsible for maintaining local roads.

towns is made up of judges known as lay magistrates. They have powers similar to those of judges in the United States and Canada. These are the lowest courts, and their judgments may be overturned by a higher court.

Towns and villages are responsible for local roads and transportation. The police, firefighters, water services, electricity, and schools are also taken care of by the municipality. All these services cost money, however, so the municipal government collects taxes, too. These taxes vary greatly from one community to another, depending on the needs of the region.

A Center for Peace

Since the nineteenth century, Switzerland has been a center for world organizations and international peace talks. The biggest reason for this, of course, is the country's neutrality, and their commitment to promoting peace. (Conveniently for all involved in these organizations and talks, it is also one of the world's loveliest places to go for a convention!) These meetings began in the 1800s with the International Working Men's Association. This was the first effort to organize an international labor movement, and it succeeded. The group later became known as the International Labor Organization (ILO), with headquarters in Geneva.

The European headquarters of the United Nations in Geneva

After World War I, U.S. President Woodrow Wilson recommended Geneva as the center for the League of Nations.

In 1945, the United Nations (UN) replaced it and still has many of its offices in Geneva. Important peace talks have been conducted here, including the Nuclear Nonproliferation Treaty of 1968, and the Reagan-Gorbachev talks of 1985, which ended in increased weapons control.

The city was also the site of an important series of talks concerning the Middle East and the Organization of Petroleum Exporting Countries (OPEC). Peace talks during the Persian Gulf War and other Middle Eastern crises also took place in Geneva.

Many other international organizations also have their headquarters in this city. The World Health Organization—the leading agency for preventing infectious diseases—has its base here. Geneva is also host to the Office of the High Commission for Refugees, European Center for Nuclear Research, World Meteorological Organization, International Telecommunications Union, World Scout Bureau, International Council of Osteopaths, and the World Intellectual Property Organization (which protects patents and copyrights), to name just a few.

Women's Firsts in Swiss Government

Elisabeth Kopp (1936-)

In 1984, Elisabeth Kopp (right), from Lucerne, was the first woman elected to the Swiss Federal Council. She served until 1988 and today, practices law in the same law firm as her husband.

Ruth Dreifus (1940-)

Ruth Dreifus (below right) was elected Switzerland's first woman President and Chairman of the National Council in 1999. She is from the town of Edingen and represents Geneva. Following her year as President, she became Minister of the Department of Home Affairs, which is similar to the U.S. Department of the Interior.

Trix Heberlein (1942-)

In 1999, Trix Heberlein was elected President of the Federal Assembly, a position like Speaker of the House of Representatives in the United States.

Overcoming the Odds

72

FOR A SMALL, SHELTERED COUNTRY LYING BETWEEN THE JURA Mountains and the Alps, Switzerland's economy is outstanding. The country is at a disadvantage agriculturally, unable to farm much of its mountainous land. The mountains also made trade with other countries more difficult, especially before tunnels were cut through the mountain passes. But these drawbacks have not stopped Switzerland from becoming one of the wealthiest countries in the world, with a solid economic base. Their dedication to perfection and service made the Swiss leaders in tourism, banking, and fine products.

Opposite: **Farming in a mountain valley**

The Swiss Franc

The official abbreviation of the Swiss franc is CHF. One hundred *Rappen* equal one franc. Modern coins include denominations of the *Rappen* and franc, and paper currency comes in 10, 20, 50, 100, 200, 500 and 1000 francs. Subjects pictured on Swiss currency often represent areas of Swiss culture and the arts. Political leaders are rarely shown, although the Swiss national hero, William Tell, has been pictured. Scientific subjects, such as space discoveries or images of nature, are also shown.

Harvesting grapes

$$\text{Farming a Difficult Landscape}$$

The soil and conditions of alpine land are not suited for crops, so most of Switzerland's grassy land is used to graze cattle. The most common crops are fruits, including grapes in areas that get a lot of sun, as well as potatoes, wheat, and other grains. In the Ticino canton, olive trees flourish.

All the farming is done on the Swiss Plateau, with farmland taking up only about 10 percent of the land area. The average farm covers about 8 acres (3 hectares), so farmers take care of the soil in order to get the most out of their land. They seek to avoid the problems that farmers face in other parts of the world because of overuse of farmlands.

This small farm production means that the nation does not grow enough food to feed all its people, so 60 percent of Switzerland's food is imported. Dependence upon food imports puts an economic strain on any country.

The forests of Switzerland cover about 25 percent of the land. However, the Swiss protect this relative abundance of trees. Strict pollution controls have been imposed on automobiles to prevent any further damage to the forests.

About forty percent of the land is used for grazing cattle, which make up a large part of the nation's agriculture. In 1997, Switzerland had 1.76 million cattle, producing not only

Cattle are an important part of Swiss agriculture.

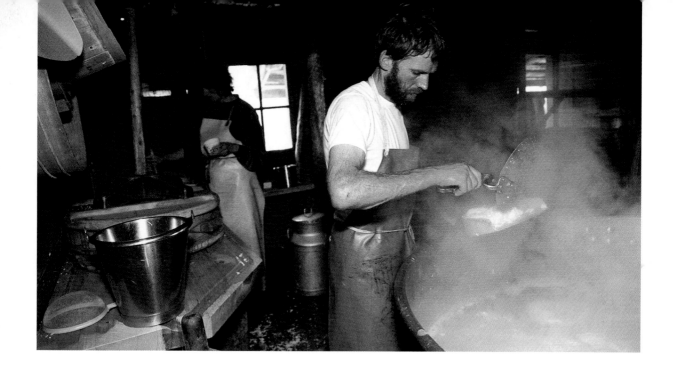

Gruyère cheese production

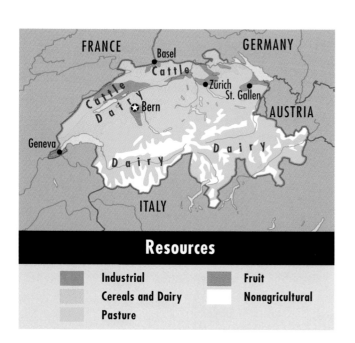

Resources

■ Industrial	■ Fruit
■ Cereals and Dairy	□ Nonagricultural
■ Pasture	

beef products, but also the milk and cheeses that Switzerland is famous for. Emmentaler, for example, is a favorite, better known in North America as "Swiss cheese." Other livestock includes chickens, pigs, sheep, and also goats that produce milk for cheeses.

The warmer Ticino canton is known for its olives and the production of fine salamis and cheeses. This region also produces popular wines. The cantonal government of Ticino recognized the importance of this industry and developed a strictly regulated and respected system to promote a high quality of wine. Merlot is the specialty of the region.

Switzerland's natural resources are not abundant in the conventional sense. Although its mountains built the extensive tourism industry, the land offers very little in the way of underground resources. Salt is the only important mineral mined here. Timber was once a source of revenue, but environmental concerns have prevailed. Hydroelectric power is probably the nation's best resource, because it is renewable, free, and clean. Most factories in Switzerland are powered by the rivers that flow from the mountains.

A worker in a salt mine

What Switzerland Grows, Makes, and Mines

Agriculture

Dairy products	3,900,000 metric tons
Livestock	3,135,000 head
Fruit and vegetables	2,027,000 metric tons
Cereal grains	988,000 metric tons

Manufacturing (value in Swiss francs)

Non-electrical machinery and vehicles	13,570,000,000
Electronics and optics	12,306,000,000
Metal products	8,241,000,000

Mining

Salt	4,000,000 metric tons

As a landlocked country with high and treacherous mountains guarding much of its border, Switzerland has had to use expensive ground transportation for both imports and exports. With its lack of natural resources, self-sufficiency has always been a challenge.

The backbone of Switzerland's economic success is quality. The Swiss realized that if they created lightweight, high-quality products that were easy to transport, they could make a good profit. Because of this, most Swiss exports are small and expensive, but among some of the most highly respected products in the world.

One of the most well-known Swiss products is watches. The popular—and expensive—Rolex watches are made here. To illustrate the economic advantage of small, high-quality pieces, compare the cost of materials with the cost of labor.

Computer-aided watch design

The metals and parts needed to make a watch cost only 5 percent of what it costs to pay the watchmaker. This means that a great deal of the money stays in Switzerland, instead of going back out to buy more materials. Swiss manufacturing also includes other precision instruments, such as electrical equipment, machine tools, and chemicals. About 45 percent of the country's exports are products from the machine and metalwork industries. Textiles are another major industry. As the first major production industry in Switzerland, it was a vital source of income in the 1800s and has continued to be important.

Today, Swiss scientists and researchers are considered among the best in the world. A recent survey by *Science Magazine* ranked Swiss researchers in immunology, molecular biology, pharmacology, and physics first place around the world, and second in astrophysics, biochemistry, chemistry, and microbiology.

Aluminum packaging is one of Switzerland's metal industries.

Trading with the World

Switzerland's largest trading partners are Western Europe and the United States. In 1994, Switzerland exported products worth U.S.$69.6 billion. This trade was split between Western Europe (63 percent), the United States (9 percent), and Japan (3 percent). By 1997, Swiss exports to the United States had increased by 25 percent. The nation's exports are almost equal to its imports, because the people need more products than the country can produce. Imports in 1994 were U.S.$68.2 billion. Most imports came from Western Europe (79.2 percent), and the rest from the United States (7.9 percent in 1997).

Importing Labor

Swiss industry faces a problem that few countries have— Switzerland does not have enough people to fill all the jobs. As a result, workers are brought in from other countries, especially Italy. These foreign workers—over 900,000 of them—make up 20 percent of the labor force. Many foreigners work in manufacturing and construction or service-related jobs. Service is Switzerland's most important industry, led by banking and tourism.

Swiss Banks

A Swiss bank account is known worldwide as the best place to put money, especially for those who wish to hide it. In the past, one of the most attractive elements of a Swiss bank account was anonymity, or secrecy. Only the account holder

Switzerland and the European Union

By a very close vote, Swiss citizens rejected a move by their government to join the European Economic Community (EEC), now called the European Union. The Swiss fear losing their independence if they join such efforts to blend all Europe into a single economy. It is too soon to know if the nation's economic and banking importance will be threatened by their independence. Because most of Switzerland's trade is with its European neighbors, many Swiss fear that remaining separate from the European Union will cut Switzerland off from its trading partners now that these other countries can trade with each other more freely.

and one or two other people know the secret number that identifies the owner of the account. The person's identity is so well guarded that anyone who broke this confidence could be put in jail or be fined a great deal of money. In 1991, however, total anonymity was abolished, although secrecy remains an important asset of Swiss banks. Swiss banks are also popular for political reasons. Because the country is always neutral, their banking system is less likely to be disturbed or lose money due to war or political uprising.

Europe's Playground

Tourism has been a major industry in Switzerland for the last 200 years. The beautiful scenery speaks for itself, but the Swiss people try to make sure their country is a perfect place to visit. Resorts have been built to accommodate skiers and sightseers, and Swiss inns and hotels are famous worldwide for their warm hospitality. Tourists bring in more than U.S. $11 million each year.

Switzerland is also a haven for the wealthy. Movie stars and other celebrities go to Switzerland, not only for the beautiful

Skiers in Gstaad

scenery, skiing, and shopping, but also to get away. The Swiss respect the privacy of their well-known guests. In Gstaad, for example, you may see famous movie stars talking with friends in cafes with no one else paying any attention to them.

More than 200 ski schools operate in Switzerland, with over 4,000 instructors. The Alps are among the world's most popular mountains, partially for the mystique that has carried over from the early days of English climbers hoping to conquer peaks like the Matterhorn. Summer visitors can find more than 30,000 miles (48,000 km) of marked trails for hiking. Botanical and geological study trails run through reserves, and the Alpine Mountain Club maintains 160 mountain huts for hikers.

Water sports are another tourist attraction. Canoeing and rafting are popular sports on the Inn, Saane, Rhine, Simme, and

Rhone Rivers. Switzerland's magnificent caves and glacial formations also awe tourists. Another growing industry is health spas. Many natural mineral and hot springs have particular health benefits. Over 150 health spas and 250 mineral springs claim to relieve everything from stomachaches to arthritis.

In a country full of natural wonders and people dedicated to preserving their way of life, it is no wonder tourism is Switzerland's most important industry.

Some tourists enjoy rafting on the Rhine River.

Gleis 1
Spiez-Thun-Bern
Lötschberg-Italien
Zweisimmen-Montreux

LAKEN WEST

This train station is part of Switzerland's well-organized transportation system.

Getting Around

Switzerland's geography and its tourism industry have resulted in one of the most extensive and well-organized transportation systems in the world. The nation has 3,262 miles (5,249 km) of railroads as well as 44,200 miles (71,117 km) of paved highways. For boat transportation, there are 40 miles (65 km) of artificial inland waterways. Also, boats carry passengers and cargo on Switzerland's major lakes, and along some of its rivers.

More than 13 billion passengers pass through Switzerland's five airports each year. Geneva and Zürich have international airports where Swissair serves 40 countries. Basel, where the Rhine River connects Switzerland to the North Sea, is the nation's only port.

Trains, Tunnels, and Passes

Except for a few small private lines, the railroads are owned and operated by the government. Traveling on Switzerland's railroads and roads over its steep, treacherous mountainsides is a remarkable experience.

Many passes through the mountains were established by early invaders. The Simplon Pass, which became a highway in the early 1800s, was used by Napoléon. At the Oberalp Pass, a cross bears the inscription: *Ex montibus salus*, which means "All good comes from the mountains."

The St. Gotthard Railway Tunnel

"So that the St. Gotthard Railway can meet the demands on a great international line, its culmination point should not lie higher than 1,162 meters (3,812 feet) above sea level. The smallest radius of the curves shall not be less than 300 meters (985 feet) and the steepest gradient not more than 25 per mile. The line from Flüelen to Biasca shall be built with double track and the tunnels are to be constructed for two-track operation."

This resolution was passed on October 13, 1869, by the delegations of the North German Confederation, the Grand Duchy of Baden, the Kingdom of Italy, the Kingdom of Württemberg, and the Swiss Confederation. Thanks to this farsighted decision, the St. Gotthard Railway is still of great international importance. With the smaller curve radii and steeper gradients that many people suggested, it could not be used today by all types of international trains.

This unusual tunnel makes three complete loops in order to climb the steep pass. It rises in a giant spiral inside the mountain, emerging at each turn to overlook the tiny town below from greater and greater heights.

While some railway lines tunnel through the mountains, others go right up the mountainside. The oldest cogwheel railway in Europe is at the top of Mount Rigi, reaching 5,896 feet (1,797 m) from Vitznau. The world's steepest cogwheel railway, boasting a maximum slope of 48 percent, is on Mount Pilatus. The town of Erstfield is called "railway man's village," because the long, steep climb up to the St. Gotthard Pass starts here. The highest bridge in this line is 256 feet (77 m) high.

Even more remarkable than finding a pass through the mountains is creating one. The St. Gotthard Road Tunnel is the longest highway tunnel in the world at 10.14 miles (16.31 km). When it was opened in 1882, it not only provided transportation for tourists and passengers, but also opened the Ticino canton to industry by connecting it with the rest of Switzerland.

Other tunnels through the Alps include the Lôtschberg Tunnel and the Simplon Tunnel. The Simplon Tunnel is one of the longest tunnels in the world, at 12.3 miles (19.8 km). The Great St. Bernard Tunnel, completed in 1964, was the first automobile tunnel through the Alps.

The Swiss public-transportation system is one of the most advanced and well-organized in Europe. Trains and buses are impeccably clean and run on time (all the conductors have Swiss watches, of course!). The William Tell Express is a unique example of Swiss ingenuity. It runs over both water and land—and then passes through the St. Gotthard Tunnel.

As the boat passengers arrive at the shore, their luggage is taken aboard the train waiting at the dock, and in no time they are rushing past the landscape toward the Alps. This line brings passengers from the upper end of Lake Lucerne all the way to Lugano on the southern toe of the Ticino. The efficiency of the Swiss transportation systems includes perfect connections between different types of transportation so that tourists don't have to wait three hours for a bus, or walk 2 miles (3.2 km) to the nearest station.

Communication

Switzerland has more than 400 newspapers, and 90 of them are published daily. Most of these publications are printed in the language of the region. Zürich's major papers, written in German, are *Der Blick*, *Tages Anzeiger Zürich*, and *Neue Züricher Zeitung*. A few non-daily papers are published in the

Newspapers in many languages at a newsstand

Romansh language. Most radio and television stations are run by the government, and all four languages are represented, although few are in Romansh. Several radio stations are privately owned, but the government controls and regulates the postal, telegraph, and telephone systems. As with all things Swiss, these are very dependable.

One Country, Four Languages

SWITZERLAND IS THE MELTING POT THAT NEVER BOILED. Its blend of cultures has mixed in a way that allows each region to keep its own ways and take pride in its individuality. Recognizing one another as Swiss, citizens from the far corners of the country (which aren't so far) still know that the differences are many. Today these differences are celebrated and enjoyed instead of fought over, as in the past.

In a 1998 estimate, there were 7,374,000 people living in Switzerland. Seventeen percent of the people are under the age of 15, and almost 15 percent are older than 65. The average life expectancy for women in Switzerland is just over 82 years. Men have a life expectancy of about 75 years. About 20 percent of this population are foreign-born, and came to Switzerland to work. About 60 percent of the residents live in an urban area. The estimated population for the year 2003 is 7,559,000.

In 1994, the literacy rate was 100 percent—the best in the world. All children are required to attend elementary school, but the specific requirements are determined by each canton individually. The

Opposite: **Boys in Saint-Moritz**

This man lives in a French-speaking region of Switzerland.

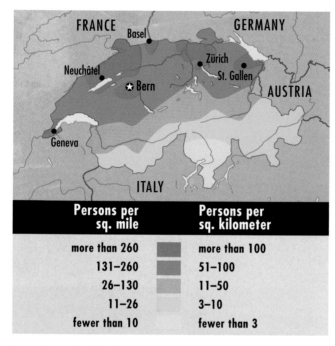

Persons per sq. mile		Persons per sq. kilometer
more than 260		more than 100
131–260		51–100
26–130		11–50
11–26		3–10
fewer than 10		fewer than 3

Population distribution
in Switzerland

Zürich canton's educational plan, which follows, is one example.

Elementary School

All Swiss children have to attend the first eight or nine years of school, which make up elementary school, called *Volksschule* in German, the predominant language of Zürich. Kindergarten, or preschool, is optional. Elementary school is divided into two sections. The first six years are similar to first through sixth grade in the United States and Canada, with one teacher for all of the subjects.

Schoolgirls after class

The second stage of elementary school lasts three years in Zürich. This part of school prepares the student for the next level of education. During this time, the students decide what type of school they would like to go to next or whether they want to learn a trade. Children in Switzerland must decide their life's path much younger than in many other places, often in their early teens. Classes are divided among three levels, depending on the student's learning ability and career goals.

At the basic level, students get the most attention. This level is geared especially toward students who have learning problems.

At the intermediate level, a variety of topics are taught, usually by two teachers per class. Students must learn one foreign language (French in the German-speaking cantons and German in the French-speaking cantons). They have the option to study a second language, usually Italian or English. Among other subjects are geography, math, history, physical-fitness, and home-economics courses such as cooking and sewing.

At the highest level, the same subjects are taught but at a greater depth. A second foreign language is much more likely, and the subjects are taught more quickly. This level must be completed in order to get into some trades and most secondary schools.

Secondary School

Some secondary schools accept students right out of primary school, but these are different from both the other secondary schools and the second stage of elementary school. They are called secondary schools of ancient languages. These students

Who Lives in Switzerland?	
German	65%
French	18%
Italian	10%
Romansh	1%
Other	6%

study some math and science, but they mainly focus on Latin and at least two other languages. A student who wants to become a doctor must go to this type of school, and it is required for a few other professions, too. Since most children start primary school at the age of seven, a student must make this important decision at the age of thirteen.

Teenagers hanging out in town

A coed basketball game

Those who have completed secondary school and have decided not to learn a trade, go to another type of school. There are three options. The first focuses more on math and science, and the second specializes in modern languages but includes other subjects. The third option is an economics school, a practical choice for anyone who would like to go into the banking industry.

Students at secondary schools receive the Federal Graduation Diploma after completing the 4 1/2 year course. This is like a high-school diploma in the United States.

Some teens in Switzerland and other European countries work as apprentices.

Students who choose not to go on to a secondary school begin their apprenticeship. The young person must now decide on a future trade or profession—usually at the age of fifteen or sixteen. The apprenticeship lasts two to four years, depending on the job.

During that time, students learn everything about the trade. Sometimes larger companies have special classes for apprentices. Many apprenticeships are less formal, especially for such jobs as hairdresser, seamstress, baker, plumber, and other trades. Some go on to technical colleges to gain a deeper knowledge of their field.

Another choice for those who took an apprenticeship but do not want to go right to work in that field, is the secondary educational path. These students can go to a school that gives a diploma very much like one given by a secondary school. The student then has the option of going to a university like any student with a Federal Graduation Diploma.

Universities and Technical Colleges

The universities in Switzerland are divided into technical and nontechnical schools. The universities run by the federal government tend to be in more technical fields, while those run by the cantons focus on nontechnical subjects. The average university course takes 4 1/2 years. Switzerland has eight canton-run universities as well as the Confederation's Swiss Federal Institutes of Technology.

Technical colleges are similar to the Swiss Federal Institutes of Technology, but are not quite so advanced. The advantage for those who attend one of these schools is that they have likely already finished an apprenticeship in their field, which means that their hands-on skills are much better than those who have only studied in a classroom. There are 23 technical colleges in Switzerland. Students attending technical college full time complete their studies in 3 1/2 years. Those who need to work while attending school may attend a six-year night-school program.

A Land of Many Tongues

Switzerland has four official languages. The most widely spoken of these is German. French is the next most common language, and Italian is spoken mainly in Ticino canton. The fourth language—Romansh—is spoken by only 1 percent of the people and is

Population of Switzerland's Major Cities (1996)	
Zürich	343,869
Basel	174,007
Geneva	173,559
Bern	127,469
Lausanne	115,878

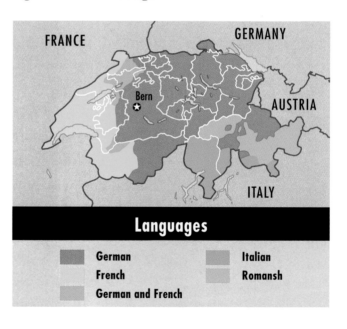

Pronouncing the Languages

German, French, and Italian letters are pronounced much the same as they are in English. There are big differences, however. The biggest difference in German is ü, which is pronounced like the letter u in English, but with lips pursed as they would be for a kiss or a whistle. The closest sound in English would be the ue in "fuel."

In French, the letter u has no English equivalent. Round your lips as if to pronounce the letter o, then say ee. The French letter ç is pronounced like an s in English. In Italian, when the letter c is followed by an e or an i, it is pronounced like the English dipthong ch. When it is followed by an h, it is pronounced like the c in "cat."

The Many Languages of Switzerland

Total Population:

German	65%
French	18%
Italian	12%
Romansh	1%
Other	4%

Swiss Citizens Only:

German	74%
French	20%
Italian	4%
Romansh	1%
Other	1%

very closely related to Latin. The language of each region reflects the ethnic backgrounds of the people and is part of what keeps them unique.

Most cantons have an official language that is used by its government and taught in schools. The signs of most small businesses are in that language, and you would usually hear it spoken on the street, too. Many places use the multiple languages, however, especially larger towns and cities where tourists of all nationalities often go. Bigger restaurants have multilingual menus, for instance, and place names are posted in each language.

Most of the German spoken by the people of Switzerland is a dialect specific to Swiss speakers called Swiss-German. Formal German is used in newspapers, television, and other official business, however.

The government requires that all product labeling, national broadcasting, and major highway signs be printed in German, French, and Italian. Things can get a little crowded on a pocket-sized package of peanuts! The federal government takes the issue of language so seriously, that it requires each

Défense de traverser les voies
Überschreiten der Gleise verboten
Vietato traversare i binari
Do not cross the railway lines

This warning sign is in French, German, Italian, and English.

language group to be represented in the Federal Tribunal. This attention to equality is recognized as important in keeping the peace and making sure that everyone feels and is heard.

Switzerland is only place in the world where the archaic Romansh language is still spoken. It resembles Latin, and is spoken by about 50,000 people in the canton of Graubünden, especially in Engadine and Grisons Oberland. Although only 1 percent of the Swiss people speak Romansh, it was recognized as a fourth official language in 1938. This was accomplished by the Romansh league, which has worked hard to preserve this old language.

Religion and Beliefs: More Diversity

S WITZERLAND'S RELIGIOUS PAST HAS BEEN FULL OF CHALlenges and disagreements. After all the years of religious arguments, however, the Swiss realized that they must solve these differences to live peacefully. Today, Switzerland has complete religious freedom. The two major religious groups in Switzerland today are the Protestants and the Catholics. These two faiths divide the country nearly in half, but only in numbers. People of both faiths live side by side in total peace and cooperation—although religion is not a welcome topic for casual conversation.

Religions of Switzerland	
Roman Catholic	48%
Protestant	44%
Other	8%

Not Always Churchgoers

In Switzerland, claiming a religion does not necessarily include attending church regularly—or ever. A person's religion is often considered to be that of their family, even if they have not gone to church for two generations. Many people who do not attend church regularly still observe the ceremonial rites. Babies are baptized in church, couples are married in church, and the dead are buried in church ceremonies.

A village church

Religion and Beliefs: More Diversity **99**

Christmas Traditions

Christmas traditions vary from region to region, but Christmas is traditionally a quiet holiday, a time for families. Like other religious holidays in Switzerland, it is celebrated over two days, with further festivities on Saint Stephen's Day, December 26. In villages, the celebration begins with the arrival at each house of the *Christkindli*, a girl dressed in white, wearing a veil and crowned in gold and jewels. She and her helpers, children dressed in white, arrive on a sleigh pulled by reindeer. Their arrival at each house is the signal to light the Christmas tree. After everyone sings a carol around the tree, gifts are distributed to the family's children from the large basket the *Christkindli* carries.

On Christmas Eve, only the pealing of church bells breaks the silence. The church bells in the large city of Zürich have filled the cold winter air with joyful sounds for hundreds of years. These bells are played on radio and in recordings all over the world. In the Valais canton, Christmas Eve is also the time for community bell-ringing contests.

Carolers sometimes go from house to house singing the old songs. In Zürich, processions of costumed children, carrying cowbells and other noisemakers, parade from house to house expecting small treats, much as North American children do at Halloween.

Swiss children caroling outdoors

The Legend of Devil's Stone

Legend says that once upon a time, the devil built a bridge in three days for the people of Göschenen over the chasm of Schöllenen Gorge. But when the devil asked for the sacrifice of a human soul and got a goat instead, he became very angry and wanted to destroy the bridge. Today, pictures of an outraged devil are depicted on a stone beside the bridge as a reminder.

Because Switzerland was created by so many different groups, it has no unified mythology or spiritual legacy from its ancient peoples. The Swiss in general are not superstitious. Their folk legends revolve more around historical events.

Several places in the Alps have become pilgrimage centers—places where people go to pray for special favors or to celebrate a saint's day. The little town of Einsiedeln in

Schwyz canton is dominated by a beautiful Benedictine abbey, where a statue of the Madonna is believed to work miracles. Another pilgrimage church, Madonna del Sasso, stands high on a rock overlooking the Catholic city of Locarno, in Italian-speaking Switzerland. Swiss Catholics also go to Sachseln, on the shore of Lake Sarnen, to visit the tomb of the country's patron saint, Nicholas of Flüe.

The Benedictine abbey in Einsiedeln

Leaders of Reform

Ulrich Zwingli (1484–1531), a Catholic priest, disagreed with many practices of the Roman Catholic Church in the sixteenth century. He believed that priests should be able to marry, and he opposed fasting and the worship of saints. But his biggest criticism was the sale of indulgences—blessings by the pope (the leader of the Roman Catholic Church) that were supposed to increase a person's chance of going to heaven after death. Zwingli objected to the fact that some priests were capitalizing on the indulgences. Instead of giving the blessings freely to good people in their congregation, these corrupt priests were charging money for them. And Zwingli saw that this custom was increasing.

Despite his good intention of protecting people from this unfairness, Zwingli was supported by only about half of Switzerland's Catholics. He then decided to form his own church, a branch of Protestantism, and gathered a number of followers.

John Calvin (1509–1564) was born in Noyon, France. His father was a lawyer for the Roman Catholic Church. Calvin's studies brought him to Paris, where he concentrated on Greek and Latin. Here he was heavily influenced by the new ideas of the Renaissance.

In 1533, Calvin declared himself Protestant, and the next year he settled in Basel, Switzerland. This was during a time of religious tension between Swiss Catholics and Protestants. Calvin published a book called the *Institutes of the Christian Religion* (1536), which he kept working on for the rest of his life. This book and his preaching were also influential in England, Scotland, and colonial North America. His strict beliefs strongly influenced the Puritans. In 1536, Calvin became the leader of the first organization of Protestant pastors in Geneva, but he was banished two years later for having doctrines that were too strict.

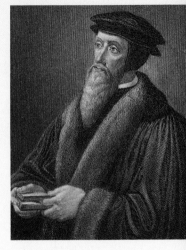

During his time in Geneva, he had been not only a preacher, but also an administrator and a popular speaker. As a local leader, he inspired people's respect. After Calvin left the city, his Protestant organization declined and they soon asked him to come back. Three years after being asked to leave, the preacher went back to live in Geneva, and remained popular there until his death.

A Good Climate for Culture

OUTDOOR ACTIVITIES HAVE ALWAYS BEEN IMPORTANT to the Swiss, and their enthusiasm for walking, hiking, and skiing may have developed from the harsh realities of survival in a cold, rugged landscape. But the climate has also encouraged a flourishing of the arts, and since their earliest days the Swiss have considered music and fine arts important.

Switzerland's art history goes back to the architecture of the Romans, who left their mark all over the land. Ruins of their great buildings remain at Augst, Windisch, Avenches, Martigny, and Orbe. At Avenches in the first and second centuries, the Romans built an arena that seated 10,000 people. Riva San Vitale has an octagonal fifth-century baptistery, and Müstair has wonderful examples of churches from the time of Charlemagne. A church at Zillis has the oldest wooden ceiling with painted figures in the western world.

Opposite: **Skiers enjoy Switzerland's marvelous slopes**

The oldest painted wooden ceiling in the western world

Old cathedrals with vaulted ceilings and beautiful ornamentation can be found in Zürich, Bern, Basel, Schaffhausen, and Geneva. Monasteries with the swirling gold flourishes of the baroque period of architecture offer a slice of history in Disentis, Engelberg, and Einsiedeln. The Abbey of St. Gall is another fine example of baroque architecture.

The Daydream by Ferdinand Hodler

Switzerland is also home to many modern artists. Among these nineteenth and twentieth century artists are Max Bill, Jean Arp, Meret Oppenheim, Paul Klee, and Ferdinand Hodler. In 1916, the modern artistic movement called dadaism was founded by Swiss artists. Sculptors Alberto Giacometti and Jean Tugley are well known worldwide. The works of many Swiss artists are displayed at the Museum of Fine Arts in Bern. Bern also has a Museum of Natural History and a collection of Swiss textiles at the Abegg Foundation at Riggisberg. Zürich has a museum of fine arts, too, and the Swiss National Museum there contains many historical artifacts. The Rietberg Museum has a collection of non-European art and artifacts.

The modern Swiss artist with the most long-lasting legacy to the world was the architect Le Corbusier. His real name was Charles-Èdouard Jeanneret, and he is considered the father of modern urban architecture.

Jean-Jacques Rousseau

Jean-Jacques Rousseau (1712–1778) was a highly influential writer, a pioneer in the romantic movement of literature. He was born in Geneva in 1712. He lost his mother at birth, and his father, who was a watchmaker, was exiled when Jean-Jacques was ten. Mostly self-educated with books his father had introduced him to, Rousseau was unhappy living with his uncle and learning to be an engraver. In March 1728, at only sixteen years old, the boy suddenly left Geneva. He traveled through his own country, as well as France and Italy.

As he grew older, Rousseau continued to study on his own, becoming absorbed in literature and writing. By 1750, he had settled in Paris and was beginning to be recognized for his work as a writer of essays, plays, and operas. During this time he called himself a "citizen of Geneva."

On June 9, 1762, the Parliament of Paris issued a warrant for Rousseau's arrest, and ten days later, two of his works, *Emile* and *The Social Contract* were burned and banned. People in power in Paris had been outraged at his pleas for civil liberties, his dislike of widespread corruption, and his ideas for new government. One of his most famous quotes, the first line of *Emile*, sums up his point of view: "God makes all things good; man meddles with them and they become evil."

Rousseau left Paris, but persecution for his ideas and beliefs in freedom and human rights followed wherever he went. Finally he was allowed to return to Paris, where he spent the last eight years of his life working on his autobiography. His works, especially his *Confessions*, were revolutionary for their time as self-reflective works that deal with the creation and formation of the human soul.

Literature

Most major Swiss literature is written in German. Since literature is classified by the language it is written in, much of Swiss literature is listed as German.

Johanna Spyri's novel *Heidi* is one of the best-known tales to come from Switzerland. It is the story of a little orphan girl sent to live with her hermit grandfather high on a mountain in the Alps. How she brightens his life and eventually causes her grandfather to make peace with the townspeople of Dörfli has made Heidi an ambassador of Alpine life and values for much of the world. The book has been translated into more than 40 languages and made into plays, movies, television productions, and even an opera.

Shirley Temple appeared in the 1937 film, *Heidi*.

Although Dörfli was not a real town, Johanna Spyri based her descriptions on three towns in the Graubünden canton near the Liechtenstein border—Maienfeld, Cuscha, and Ober Rofels. Maienfeld today has a fountain with a statue of Heidi and a walking trail that follows sites mentioned in the book.

Other major Swiss writers include Jeremias Gotthelf, Conrad Ferdinand Meyer, and Gottfried Keller. In 1919, Carl Spitteler won the Nobel Prize for his epics and other literary works.

An Underground Wonder

In 1549, someone first had the idea of building underground mills, and in 1651, the dream became a reality. Named the Col-des-Roches Mills, the system included waterwheels, flour mills, threshing machines, and sawmills. The mills were in operation for 250 years, until they closed down in 1898 and were almost forgotten. While these underground mills were unused, they slowly filled with garbage and mud. In 1973, a group of volunteers decided to clean them out so that the public could see the work done so long ago. But before they closed, the mills were made immortal by Danish writer Hans Christian Andersen, who wrote: "We find ourselves . . . in an underground mill. Deep under the earth rushes a river; above no-one dreams that it is there. . . . O, will you love these mills, as I love you!"

Music

Switzerland has a far richer musical heritage than the stereotypical yodeling and alphorns. Opera, jazz, and popular music are enjoyed in the busy concert and theatre season lasting from September to May. In summer, music festivals are popular with both locals and tourists. The major festivals are held in Lausanne, Zürich, Thun, Meiringen, Braunwald, Interlaken, and Lucerne. Geneva's *Orchestre de la Suisse Romande* is a symphony orchestra made famous under conductor Ernest Ansermet.

Along with its music festivals, Switzerland is well known for its international film festivals at Locarno and Les Dialerets and for the Rose d'Or Festival at Montreaux. Summer highlights for many visitors are the performances of the legend of William Tell, in Friedrich Schiller's *Wilhelm Tell*, at Altdorf and Interlaken.

Performers at an outdoor concert in Zürich

Yodelers in traditional dress

Alphorns can be heard over long distances in the mountains.

Of course, yodeling and the alphorn are also part of Swiss music, having been used to communicate over long distances in the mountains. The alphorn was used by cattle herdsmen, and yodeling imitates the rising and falling echoes of voices calling in the mountains.

Snowboarding

Winter Means Sports

One-third of the Swiss people ski, and over 90,000 belong to the Alpine Mountain Club. Members can be as young as ten years old. Along with skiing down mountainsides, the Swiss enjoy cross-country skiing, bobsledding, tobogganing, snowboarding, and *skijöring*. This unusual sport involves riding on skis across a frozen lake or flat meadow, pulled by a galloping horse.

The Alpine slopes and their ample snowfalls have made Switzerland a paradise for skiers. Add to that the Swiss talent as hotel keepers and hosts, and you have Europe's major winter resort region. Zermatt, under the beautiful silhouette of the Matterhorn, is perhaps the most famous of all, a picture-postcard Swiss village.

A rock climber

In the summer, the Swiss are just as keen on outdoor sports. They enjoy climbing, hiking, bicycling, swimming, boating, river rafting, horseback riding, and team sports such

Hornussen is played only in Switzerland.

as soccer and *Hornussen*. Hornussen is played by two teams swinging 8-foot (2.4-m) wooden clubs. The game resembles baseball, but uses a wooden disk for a ball. Fielders catch the disk with wooden rackets.

Martina Hingis

Martina Hingis, born in 1980, was playing the sport that would bring her fame by the age of two. Tennis seemed to be a part of her, ever since her parents named her after the well-known tennis star Martina Navratilova. Born in Kosice, in what was then Czechoslovakia, the young athlete moved to Switzerland with her family when she was seven. When she became a Swiss citizen she had already played her first tennis tournament. In 1996, with Helena Sukova of the Czech Republic, Hingis became the youngest player ever to win a Wimbeldon event. In 1997, at 16 years old, Hingis won the Australian Open and put herself in the history books. She was the youngest person to win a Grand Slam singles championship since 1887. In 1997 she was the number-one female player in the world, winning seventy-five of eighty matches at tournaments such as the U.S. Open and Wimbledon.

Living the Good Life

114

DAY-TO-DAY LIFE IN SWITZERLAND IS MUCH LIKE DAILY life in any modern industrialized nation. On weekdays, children go to school, and their parents work. On weekends and holidays, families enjoy many of the same sports and social activities as their neighbors in Germany and France, or as Americans and Canadians do. But that's not to say that life in Switzerland is exactly like life everywhere else.

Opposite: **All around the country, people enjoy festivals.**

A family outing to a regional park

The Swiss are very serious about their jobs, and often work longer days than people in other countries. Family life is also important, though Swiss families are the smallest in the world with an average of 2.2 people in each household. Swiss people usually go to bed early, and except in the French-speaking cities of Geneva and Lausanne, nightlife is rare. Nearly every family owns a television set.

The Swiss are among some of the world's most enthusiastic newspaper readers. Switzerland's first newspaper has been in publication since 1610.

Social Life

When Swiss people meet, they greet each other by brushing cheeks three times, and they repeat this when they part. When someone enters a store, the storekeeper and the shopper greet each other. In French-speaking Switzerland, they say "*Bonjour*"; in German-speaking cantons, "*Güten Tag*"; in the Ticino canton, "*Buongiorno.*" The Swiss are very polite people and stand in line to wait their turn at cash registers, ticket windows, and bus stops. They have earned their reputation as sober, hardworking people. Social life in Switzerland revolves mainly around life's special occasions. In the mountains, the week between Christmas and New Year's Day is a time for visiting neighbors. Entire families often ski to a social gathering at a neighbor's house.

Although many Swiss do not attend church, most choose to be married there. These weddings are romantic and festive celebrations that often include a wedding procession. Parties may continue for the rest of the day and much of the night with music, dancing, and a wedding feast. The Swiss marry later than people in most countries. The average age for marriage is 27 for a woman and 29 for a man. Even total strangers wish the bride and groom good luck by honking their car horns as a bridal limousine or carriage drives past.

A baptism is also a happy event. After a short church service, guests are treated to a meal of four or five courses. And the baby is presented with gifts from all.

Funerals are also followed by meals, called funeral feasts. Relatives and friends gather to share their grief and everyone wears dark clothing to funerals.

A baptism

Wooden chalets are common in the mountains.

Chalets to Apartments

Especially in Switzerland's mountain regions, the chalet, with its overhanging roof and flower-decked balconies, is a popular style of architecture. Farmhouses in the chalet style are often quite large, but with a barn on the lower level. In areas where winter storms may rage for days, having animals in the same building is important, because farmers might be unable to reach free-standing barns through the deep snow.

Buildings in the Ticino canton are more likely to be made of stone, sometimes covered in stucco, a fine plasterlike covering. The walls of these stone buildings are usually quite thick. Even the roofs are sometimes made of stone, with flat stones laid in overlapping rows like shingles.

Many buildings in the Ticino region are built of stone.

Rural traditions are still followed in remote farming areas and high in the mountain villages. One of the most colorful is held in the spring when cattle herds are moved from their winter barns to graze on the high mountain pastures. Each animal is decorated with flowers, and wears a large deep-toned bell that will help herdsmen locate the animal in the meadows. A second procession is held when the cattle come down from the mountains in the fall.

Festivals are held in spring and fall when cattle move between summer pastures and winter barns.

City festivals often center around a historic event or a religious or patriotic holiday. Then people enjoy dancing, street revels, and food from sidewalk stalls.

A festival in Basel

Holidays and Festivals in Switzerland

New Year's Day	January 1
Berchtold's Day	January 2
Morgenstraich (traditional carnival in Basel)	Monday morning after Ash Wednesday
Good Friday, Easter, Easter Monday	March-April
Corpus Christi	April
Sechselaüten (Zürich tradition to end winter sooner)	3rd Monday in April
Labor Day	May 1
National Holiday	August 1
All Saints' Day	November 1
Christmas Day	December 25
Saint Stephen's Day	December 26
New Year's Eve	December 31

The Swiss at Dinner

Typical Swiss food is hearty, satisfying, and always based on fresh ingredients. As you might expect from a country with such an active dairy industry, many dishes feature cheese and milk. Regional differences are strong, with Italian, French, and German cooking styles influencing the menus in their regions.

The closest Switzerland comes to a national dish is *Rösti*, their delicious way of cooking potatoes. Although Rösti is made with few ingredients—potatoes, salt, cooking oil, and a little milk—it takes a skillful cook to make the potatoes brown and crisp in a golden circle without burning them.

Fondue, another popular Swiss dish, is often served as a snack after a day spent skiing. Fondue is made of melted cheese and scooped up with cubes of firm bread on a long fork.

Another melted-cheese dish enjoyed in winter is *raclette*. To make this, a large special cheese is melted over heat, then scraped off with a long knife.

Preparing cheese fondue

A Meal from Bern

A typical Bernese dish, called *Berner Platte*, combines some of the best of the region's food products. It consists of a heaping plateful of sausages, ham, smoky bacon, potatoes, green beans, and sauerkraut—a dish long used to feed hungry farmers in the middle of their long workday. A similar dish from the French-speaking canton of Vaud, *Papet a la Vaud*, combines three kinds of sausage with potatoes and onions, all cooked in wine.

Bread is served with every meal, and comes in an amazing variety. The dark breads popular in German-speaking cantons are made from whole wheat, rye, and other dark flours. *Pariserbrot*, or *Parisette*, is a long, thin, white bread served daily in French-speaking cantons, but sold everywhere. *Modelbrot* is a light bread baked in a closed mold. *Butterwecken* is a rich and buttery bread that used to be baked only on Sundays. It is sometimes braided into a loaf.

Even working mothers who don't have time for baking find time to make *Guetzli* (goodies) before Christmas for their family. Each region—even each town—has its own favorites. In Romansh-speaking Graubünden they make *Zimpt-Pitte*—cinnamon-flavored almond shortbread. People in Basel bake

Some of Switzerland's many types of bread for sale

Leckerli with almonds and honey, and in St. Gallen they make *Biberli*, little triangles stuffed with almonds and honey. *Mailänderli*, crisp golden cookies cut into star, heart, and crescent shapes, are popular everywhere.

Dr. Max Bircher-Benner

Health foods, whole grains, and fresh vegetables were popular in Switzerland long before they caught on elsewhere. This health food movement started at the clinic of Dr. Max Bircher-Benner (1867–1939), founded in Zürich in 1897. Nearly a century later, many Swiss people still follow his advice and begin each meal with an uncooked food, limit meats in their diet, and preserve vitamins by cooking vegetables for just a short time.

To Make *Bircher Muesli*

The most famous dish served at Dr. Bircher-Benner's clinic was a breakfast cereal called *Bircher Muesli*, which is now available in many places outside Switzerland. The original muesli used oatmeal, water, lemon juice, sweetened milk, apples, and almonds. But each cook prepares it differently, using the season's fresh fruit. Try this recipe:

1/4 cup quick-cooking oats (uncooked)

1/4 cup milk

1/4 cup chopped apple mixed with 1 tablespoon lemon juice

1/4 cup berries or chopped fruit

1 tablespoon slivered almonds or sunflower seeds

Mix and let stand for a few minutes before eating for breakfast or a snack. Add raisins, chopped dried apricots, other nuts, sliced bananas, or yogurt for variety.

Switzerland's long and rich history is the key to understanding the Swiss people of today. The lesson of peace was hard learned, but Switzerland is now the center for peacekeeping among nations. Their dedication to diversity and human rights is an inspiration to nations everywhere as people strive to get along despite differences.

The Swiss celebrate their differences.

Timeline

Swiss History

The French invade; the Swiss Confederation collapses.	1798
Congress of Vienna reestablishes the Swiss Confederation.	1815
Civil War; Protestants fight Catholics.	1847
Federal Swiss Constitution adopted.	1848
Red Cross established.	1863
First League of Nations session held in Geneva.	1920
Swiss remain neutral in World War II.	1939–1945
First election allowing women to vote (Basel).	1958
Switzerland joins the European Free Trade Association (EFTA).	1960
National voting rights granted to women.	1971
The 23rd canton of Jura is formed.	1979
The St. Gotthard Road Tunnel is opened.	1980
Elisabeth Kopp is the first woman elected to Federal Council.	1984
Citizens vote against becoming part of the European Union.	1992
Switzerland aids victims of war in Kosovo.	1999

World History

1865	The American Civil War ends.
1914	World War I breaks out.
1917	The Bolshevik Revolution brings Communism to Russia.
1929	Worldwide economic depression begins.
1939	World War II begins, following the German invasion of Poland.
1957	The Vietnam War starts.
1989	The Berlin Wall is torn down, as Communism crumbles in Eastern Europe.
1996	Bill Clinton is reelected U.S. president.

Fast Facts

Official name: Swiss Confederation

Capital: Bern

The Rhone River

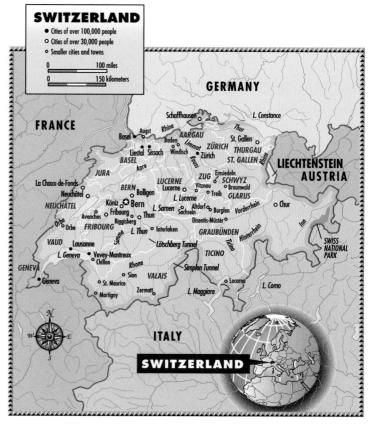

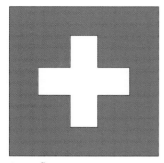

Swiss flag

Official languages:	German, French, Italian, and Romansh
Official religion:	None
Year of founding:	1648
National anthem:	"Schweizer Psalm"
Type of government:	Federal republic
Head of state:	President
Area and dimensions:	15,942 square miles (41,284 sq km)
Latitude and longitude of geographic center:	46 degrees 50 minutes north by 8 degrees 17 minutes east, just south of the village of Melchtal, in the Obwalden canton
Bordering countries:	Germany, Austria, Liechtenstein, Italy, France
Highest elevation:	Dufourspitze, 15,203 feet (4,634 m)
Lowest elevation:	Lake Maggiore shore, 633 feet (193 m)
Average temperature extremes:	Central Plateau: January, 29° to 33° F (-2° to 1° C) July, 65° to 70° F (18° to 21° C)
Average precipitation:	40-45 inches (100-114 cm)
National population (est. 1998):	7,374,000

Rafting on the Rhine River

The Bears of Bern

Currency

Population of major cities (1996 estimate):

Zürich	343,869
Basel	174,007
Geneva	173,559
Bern	127,469
Lausanne	115,878

Famous landmarks:

- ▶ **The Matterhorn**, *Zermatt*
- ▶ **Chapel Bridge**, *Lucerne*
- ▶ **The Bears of Bern**, *Bern*
- ▶ **Chillon Castle**, *Chillon*
- ▶ **Palace of Nations**, *Geneva*
- ▶ **The Rütli**, *on Lake Lucerne*

Industry: Industry in Switzerland generally imports lightweight raw materials, which are then processed to produce small, high-quality products for export. These products include watches, chemicals, pharmaceuticals, precision tools, and textiles. The service industry includes international banking and tourism. Switzerland is well known for exports of fine chocolate, cheeses, and other processed foods.

Currency: Since Switzerland has abstained from joining the European Union, the unit of currency is the franc (CHF). In 2000 the exchange rate was CHF 1.8085 = $US 1.

System of weights and measures: Metric

Literacy (1990 est.): 100%

Young skiers

Common Swiss words and phrases:

German

Güten Morgen	good morning
Güten Tag	good day
Bitte	please
danke schöen	thank you
ja	yes
nein	no

French

bonjour	good morning or good day
s'il vous plait	please
merci	thank you
oui	yes
non	no

Italian

buongiorno	good morning
per favore	please
grazie	thank you
si	yes
no	no

Famous people:

John Calvin	(1509–1564)
Protestant reformer	
Jean Henri Dunant	(1828–1910)
Founder of Red Cross	
Martina Hingis	(1980–)
Tennis champion	
Carl Jung	(1875–1961)
Psychiatrist	
Jean-Jacques Rousseau	(1712–1778)
Writer	

Martina Hingis

To Find Out More

Nonfiction

▶ Clark, Roland W. *The Alps.*
New York: Knopf, 1973.

▶ Cowie, Donald. *Switzerland:
The Land and the People.* New York:
A. S. Barnes and Company, 1971.

▶ Eu-Wong, Shirley. *Culture Shock:
Switzerland.* Portland, Oregon:
Graphic Arts Center Publishing
Company, 1996.

▶ *Peoples of the World*, Volume 8.
Danbury, Connecticut: Grolier
Publishing Co.

Fiction

▶ Spyri, Johanna. *Heidi.* Available
in many different editions.

Websites

▶ http://www.ethz.ch/swiss/Switzerland Info.html *has information on each canton, including a picture of its flag.*

▶ http://www.swissemb.org *is the Swiss Embassy's site, with the latest information on government leaders and economic statistics.*

Index

Page numbers in *italics* indicate illustrations.

Meet the Author

LURA JEANNE ROGERS first fell in love with Switzerland while she was climbing on a trail from the little village of Stechelberg, at the end of the Post Bus route from Lauterbrunnen. After what seemed like a short climb, she stopped, turned around and found herself eye-to-eye with the peak of a snowcovered Alp.

Lura had traveled in Switzerland before, the first time when she was eleven years old, and walked through a tunnel inside a glacier. On later trips, she rode across Switzerland by boat, following its lakes and rivers, with short train rides in between, from Geneva to Lucerne, and then took the "William Tell Express" by boat and train through the St. Gotthard Tunnel into the Ticino.

To learn more about Switzerland while writing and traveling, she read several books about the Alps and European history. She found current news and government information on the Swiss Embassy's site, *http://www.swissemb.org*. For current statistics, she relied on *Statistical Abstracts of the World*, and the 1999 world almanacs. She found travel guides useful for details about specific towns and sites.

Lura learned her research skills as an English major at Skidmore College. While studying there, she also worked in developing websites for professors. Among her writing credits is *Enchantment of the World: Dominican Republic*, published by Children's Press in 1999. She wrote about the states of New Hampshire and Vermont for *Frommer's America on Wheels: New York and New England*, and recently traveled to Europe to photograph the Algarve for a book, *Signpost: Portugal*.

Lura found the most enjoyable part of writing this book to be traveling in small Swiss villages and talking with local people, most of whom speak English. She now lives in Brattleboro, Vermont.

Photo Credits

Photographs ©:

Animals Animals/D. Valla/Suviv/OSF: 32;

Archive Photos: 14 (Express Newspapers), 71 bottom (Monika Flueckiger/ Reuters), 40, 52, 103 right, 107;

Art Resource, NY/Giraudon: 106;

Christie's Images: 49;

Churchill & Klehr Photography: 58, 79, 88;

Corbis-Bettmann: 57 bottom (AFP), 36 bottom, 100, 103 left;

Envision/B.W. Hoffmann: 94;

International Stock Photo: 9, 25 (Roberto Arakaki), 119 (Andre Jenny), 89 (Phyllis Picardi), 7 bottom, 65 top, 114 (Stockman), 47 (Paul Thompson), 13 (Hilary Wilkes);

John Selfridge: 12, 21, 69, 75, 84, 99, 118;

Kevin Downey Photography: 17, 28, 112;

Kobal Collection/20th Century Fox: 108;

Liaison Agency, Inc.: 113 bottom, 133 bottom (Evan Agostini), 76 top (Gilles Bassignac), 74 (Stephane Engler), 54 (Hulton Getty), 57 top (Nicolas Le Corre), 78 (Christophe Loviny), 71 top (Alain Morvan), 82 (Bertrand Rieger), 59 (Transon-Von Plant), 105 (Mathias Tugores);

National Geographic Image Collection/Jodi Cobb: 2;

North Wind Picture Archives: 36 top, 38, 41;

Peter Arnold Inc.: 110 top (Tischler Fotborafen), 15 bottom, 16 (Helmut Gritscher), 18, 83, 31 bottom (Oldrich Karasek), 7 top, 110 bottom (Malcolm S. Kirk), 64 (Bruno P. Zehnder);

Photo Researchers: 121 (Cheuva/ Explorer), 26 (Manfred Danegger/ Okapia), 109 (Sylvain Grandadam), 61, 67 bottom (Porterfield-Chickering), 11 top (Rapa/Explorer), 33 (Hans Reinhard/Okapia), 30 (St. Meyers/Okapia);

Ringier AG Dokumentation Bild: 42 (Felix Aeberli), 77 (Philippe Kramer), 113 top, 124 (Siegfried Kuhn), 29, 46 (Christian Lanz), 101 (Josef Ritler), 15 top (Albert Schnelle), 63, 126;

Stock Boston: 97 (Dean Abramson), 37 bottom (Fabian Falcon), 73, 132 bottom (David Simson);

Stone: 23 (Grilly Bernard), 120 (David Hanson), cover, 6 (Manfred Mehlig), 53 (Art Wolfe);

Superstock, Inc.: 20, 130 left;

The Image Works: 93 (Stuart Cohen), 87, 92, 102 (M. Granitsas), 70 (Marcel & Eva Malherbe), 34 (Lee Snider);

Ulrike Welsch: 8, 11 bottom, 22, 27, 90, 98, 104, 111, 115, 123, 125, 127, 133 top;

Unicorn Stock Photos/Alice M. Presott: 117;

Wolfgang Käehler: 31, 72, 132 top.

Maps by: Joe Le Monnier